GW00498411

Oṁ

THE BHAGAVADGĪTĀ
or
THE SONG DIVINE

(With Sanskrit Text and English Translation)

त्वमेव माता च पिता त्वमेव
त्वमेव बन्धुश्च सखा त्वमेव।
त्वमेव विद्या द्रविणं त्वमेव
त्वमेव सर्वं मम देवदेव॥

Gita Press, Gorakhpur
India

[534] गीता सजिल्द (अंग्रेजी) 1

Thirty-sixth Reprint 2011 15,000
Total 9,12,625

❖ Price : Rs. 12
(Twelve Rupees only)

ISBN 81-293-0243-8

Printed & Published by :

Gita Press, Gorakhpur—273005 (INDIA)
(a unit of Gobind Bhavan-Karyalaya, Kolkata)

Phone - (0551) 2334721, 2331250; Fax - (0551) 2336997
e-mail : **booksales@gitapress.org** website : **www.gitapress.org**

[534]

The Greatness of The Gītā

Truly speaking, none has power to describe in words the glory of the Gītā, for it is a book containing the highest esoteric doctrines. It is the essence of the Vedas; its language is so sweet and simple that man can easily understand it after a little practice; but the thoughts are so deep that none can arrive at their end even after constant study throughout a lifetime. Everyday they exhibit new facets of Truth, therefore they remain ever fresh and new. When scrutinized with a concentrated mind, possessed of faith and reverence, every verse of the Gītā will clearly appear as full of the deepest mystery. The manner in which the Gītā describes the virtues, glory and secrets of God, is hardly found in any other scripture; for in other books, the teachings are generally mixed up, more or less, with worldly subjects; but the Gītā uttered by the Lord is such an incomparable book that not a word will be found in it, which is devoid of some spiritual import. That is why Śrī Vedavyāsa, after describing the Gītā in the Mahābhārata, said in the end:—

गीता सुगीता कर्तव्या किमन्यैः शास्त्रविस्तरैः।
या स्वयं पद्मनाभस्य मुखपद्माद्विनिःसृता॥

The Gītā should be carefully studied, i.e., after reading the text, its meaning and idea should be gathered and held in the mind. It emanated from the lotus-like lips of Bhagavān Viṣṇu Himself, from whose navel sprung the lotus. What is the use of studying the other elaborate scriptures? Moreover, the Lord Himself also described its glory at the end of the Gītā (Vide Chapter XVIII verses 68 to 71).

All men, irrespective of Varṇa and Āśrama, possess the right to study the Gītā; the only qualifications needed are faith and reverence, for it is God's injunction to propagate the Gītā only among His devotees, and He further said that women, Vaiśyas, Śūdras and even men born of sinful wombs can attain the supreme state of salvation, if they cultivate devotion to Him. And through worship of Him by the performance of their own nature-born duties, men can attain perfection (Chapter XVIII verse 46). Reflection on these verses make it clear that all men have equal right to God-realization.

But owing to lack of understanding of the truth behind this subject, many persons who have only heard the name of the Gītā, make this assertion that the book is intended only for monks and ascetics, and they refrain from placing the book for study before their children out of fear lest through knowledge of the Gītā the latter renounce their hearths and homes and turn ascetics themselves. But they should consider the fact that Arjuna, who had, due to infatuation, prepared himself to turn away from the duty of a Kṣatriya and live on alms, being influenced by the most secret and mysterious teachings of the Gītā, lived the life of a householder all his life and performed his duties; how can that very Gītā produce this diametrically opposite result?

Therefore, men who desire their own welfare should give up this delusion and with utmost faith and reverence induce their children to study the Gītā understanding the meaning and the underlying idea of every verse, and while studying and reflecting on it themselves, should, according to the injunction of the Lord, earnestly take to spiritual practice. For obtaining this most valuable human body, it is improper to waste even a single moment of one's time in indulging in transient enjoyments, the roots of sorrow.

Principal Teachings of the Gītā

For His own realization, God has laid down in the Gītā two principal ways—(1) Sāṅkhyayoga, and (2) Karmayoga. Of these—

(1) All objects being unreal like the water in a mirage, or the creation of a dream, Guṇas, which are the products of Māyā, move in the Guṇas, understanding this, the sense of doership should be lost with regard to all activities of the mind, senses and the body (Chapter V verses 8-9), and being established ever in identity with all-pervading God, the embodiment of Truth, Knowledge and Bliss, consciousness should be

lost of the existence of any other being but God. This is the practice of Sāṅkhyayoga.

(2) Regarding everything as belonging to God, maintaining equanimity in success or failure, renouncing attachment and the desire for fruit, all works should be done according to God's behests and only for the sake of God (Chapter II verse 48; Chapter V verse 10); and, with utmost faith and reverence, surrendering oneself to God through mind, speech and body, constant meditation on God's Form with remembrance of His names, virtues and glory, should be practised (Chapter VI verse 47). This is the practice of Yoga by disinterested action.

The result of both these practices being the same, they are regarded as one in reality (Chapter V verses 4-5). But during the period of practice, they being different according to the qualifications of the Sādhaka, the two paths have been separately described (Chapter III verse 3). Therefore, the same man cannot tread both the paths at one and the same time, even as though there may be two roads to the Ganges, a person cannot proceed by both the paths at the same time. Out of these, Karmayoga cannot be practised in the stage of Sannyāsa, for in that stage renunciation of Karma in every form has been advised. The practice of Sāṅkhyayoga, however, is possible in every Āśrama, or stage of life.

If it is argued that the Lord has described Sāṅkhyayoga as synonymous with Sannyāsa, therefore, Sannyāsīs or monks alone are entitled to practise it, and not householders, the argument is untenable, because in the course of His description of Sāṅkhyayoga in Chapter II verses 11 to 30, the Lord, here and there, showed to Arjuna that he was qualified to fight, even according to that standard. If householders were ever disqualified for Sāṅkhyayoga, how could these statements of the Lord be reconciled? True, there is this special saving clause that the Sādhaka qualified for the path of Sāṅkhya should be devoid of identification with the body; for so long as there is identification of the ego with the body, the practice of Sāṅkhyayoga cannot be properly understood. That is why the Lord described the practice of Sāṅkhyayoga as difficult (Chapter V verse 6) and disinterested Karmayoga, being easier of practice, the Lord exhorted Arjuna, every now and then, to practise it, together with constant meditation on him.

यं ब्रह्मा वरुणेन्द्ररुद्रमरुतः स्तुन्वन्ति दिव्यैः स्तवै-
र्वेदैः साङ्गपदक्रमोपनिषदैर्गायन्ति यं सामगाः।
ध्यानावस्थिततद्गतेन मनसा पश्यन्ति यं योगिनो
यस्यान्तं न विदुः सुरासुरगणा देवाय तस्मै नमः॥

"We bow to that Supreme Puruṣa, Nārāyaṇa, who is extolled even by great gods like Brahmā, Varuṇa (the god of water), Indra (the god of rain),

Rudra (the god of destruction), and the Maruts (the wind-gods) through celestial hymns; whose glories are sung by those proficient in chanting the Sāmaveda through the Vedas along with the six Aṅgas (branches of knowledge auxiliary to the Vedas), Pada (division of the Vedic text into separate words), Krama and Jaṭā (particular forms of reciting the Vedas) and the Upaniṣads; who is perceived by the Yogīs by means of their mind made steady through meditation and fixed on the Lord; and whose reality is not known even to gods and Asuras."

शान्ताकारं भुजगशयनं पद्मनाभं सुरेशं
विश्वाधारं गगनसदृशं मेघवर्णं शुभाङ्गम्।
लक्ष्मीकान्तं कमलनयनं योगिभिर्ध्यानगम्यं
वन्दे विष्णुं भवभयहरं सर्वलोकैकनाथम्॥

"Obeisance to Viṣṇu, the dispeller of the fear of rebirths, the one Lord of all the regions, possessed of a tranquil form, lying on a bed of snake, from whose navel has sprung the lotus, the Lord of all celestials, the support of the universe, similar to the sky, possessed of the colour of a cloud and possessed of handsome limbs, the Lord of Lakṣmī (the Goddess of Wealth), having lotus-like eyes, and realized by Yogīs in meditation."

—Jayadayal Goyandka

Publisher's Note

As a book of scripture, the Bhagavadgītā has assumed a position of universal interest. Its teachings have gained appreciation not only in India, but far beyond its borders, Our Gītā Library alone comprises about 1400 editions of the Bhagavadgītā published in 34 different languages including 8 foreign languages. This is our humble attempt for bringing out this English edition of the Gītā in pocket-size and in a popular form. We trust it will find favour with the English-reading public. The English translation of this edition has been based on the Hindi rendering of the Gītā made by Syt. Jayadayal Goyandka appearing in the Gītā-Tattva Number of the Hindi monthly 'Kalyan', published by the Gita Press. In preparing the present English translation, the translators have made use, every now and then, of other English translations of the Gītā, and we express our grateful acknowledgement for the same.

In order to add to the utility of this small volume an introduction by Syt. Jayadayal Goyandka and a synopsis of the Gītā have been prefixed to the translation and an article by the same author bearing on the Gītā has been appended thereto.

—Publisher

Synopsis of the Gītā

No. of Verse — Subject Discussed

Chapter I entitled
"The Yoga of Dejection of Arjuna"

1—11 Description of the principal warriors on both sides with their fighting qualities.

12—19 Blowing of conches by the warriors on both sides.

20—27 Arjuna observes the warriors drawn up for battle.

28—47 Overwhelmed by infatuation, Arjuna gives expression to his faint-heartedness, tenderness and grief.

Chapter II entitled
"Sāṅkhyayoga" (the Yoga of Knowledge)

1—10 Arjuna and Śrī Kṛṣṇa discussing Arjuna's faint-heartedness.

11—30 Sāṅkhyayoga (the Yoga of Knowledge) described.

Chapter III entitled

"Karmayoga, or the Yoga of Action"

Chapter IV entitled

"The Yoga of Knowledge as well as the disciplines of Action and Knowledge"

Chapter V entitled

"The Yoga of Action and Knowledge"

Chapter VI entitled

"The Yoga of Self-control"

No. of Verse	Subject Discussed
33—36	The question of Mind-control discussed.
37—47	The fate of one who falls from Yoga; the glory of Dhyānayoga described.

Chapter VII entitled

"The Yoga of Jñāna (Knowledge of Nirguṇa Brahma) and Vijñāna (Knowledge of Manifest Divinity)"

No. of Verse	Subject Discussed
1—7	Wisdom with real Knowledge of Manifest Divinity.
8—12	Inherence of God in all objects as their Cause.
13—19	Condemnation of men of demoniacal nature and praise of devotees.
20—23	The question of worship of other gods.
24—30	Condemnation of men, who are ignorant of the glory and true nature of God, and approbation of those who know them.

Chapter VIII entitled

"The Yoga of the Indestructible Brahma"

No. of Verse	Subject Discussed
1—7	Answer to Arjuna's seven questions on Brahma, Adhyātma and Karma (Action), etc.
8—22	The subject of Bhaktiyoga discussed.
23—28	The bright and dark paths described.

No. of Verse — Subject Discussed

Chapter IX entitled "The Yoga of Sovereign Science and the Sovereign Secret."

1—6 The subject of Jñāna (Knowledge) with its glory described.

7—10 The origin of the world discussed.

11—15 Condemnation of men of the demoniacal nature, who despise God, and the method of Bhajana of men possessed of the divine nature.

16—19 Description of God, as the soul of everything, and His glory.

20—25 The fruits of worship with a motive and without motive.

26—34 The glory of Devotion practised disinterestedly.

Chapter X entitled "The Yoga of Divine Glories"

1—7 Description of God's glories and power of Yoga with the fruit of their knowledge.

8—11 Bhaktiyoga—its fruit and glory.

12—18 Arjuna offers his praises to God and prays to the Lord for a description of His glories and power of Yoga.

19—42 The Lord describes His glories and power of Yoga.

No. of Verse Subject Discussed

Chapter XI entitled
"The Yoga of the Vision of the Universal Form"

1—4 Arjuna prays to the Lord for a vision of His Universal Form.

5—8 The Lord describes His Universal Form.

9—14 The Universal Form described by Sañjaya to Dhṛtarāṣṭra.

15—31 Arjuna sees the Lord's Universal Form and offers praises to the Lord.

32—34 God describes His glory and exhorts Arjuna to fight.

35—46 Overtaken by fright, Arjuna offers praises to God, and prays for a sight of the Lord's Four-armed Form.

47—50 The Lord describes the glory of the vision of His Universal Form, and reveals to Arjuna His Four-armed, gentle Form.

51—55 The impossibility of obtaining a sight of the Four-armed Form without exclusive Devotion, which is described with its fruit.

Chapter XII entitled
"The Yoga of Devotion"

1—12 Respective merits of the worshippers

No. of Verse Subject Discussed

of God with Form and without Form, and the means of God-realization.

13—20 Marks of the God-realized soul.

Chapter XIII entitled

"The Yoga of Discrimination between the Field and the Knower of the Field"

1—18 The subject of "Field" and the Knower of the "Field", together with Knowledge.

19—34 The subject of Prakṛti and Puruṣa (Matter and Spirit) together with knowledge.

Chapter XIV entitled

"The Yoga of Division of three Guṇas"

1—4 The glory of Knowledge; evolution of the world from Prakṛti and Puruṣa.

5—18 The qualities of Sattva, Rajas and Tamas described.

19—27 Means of God-realization, and marks of the soul who has transcended the Guṇas.

Chapter XV entitled

"The Yoga of the Supreme Person"

1—6 Description of the Universe as a tree and the means of God-realization.

No. of Verse	Subject Discussed
7—11	The Jīvātmā, or individual soul.
12—15	God and His Glory described.
16—20	The perishable (bodies of all beings), the imperishable (Jīvātmā) and the Supreme Person.

Chapter XVI entitled "The Yoga of Division between the Divine and the Demoniacal Properties"

No. of Verse	Subject Discussed
1—5	The Divine and the demoniacal properties described with their fruit.
6—20	Marks of man possessed of the demoniacal properties and their damnation described.
21—24	Instruction about renouncing conduct opposed to the scriptures and exhortation to follow the scriptures.

Chapter XVII entitled "The Yoga of the Division of the Threefold Faith"

No. of Verse	Subject Discussed
1—6	Discussion on Faith and on the fate of men who perform austere penance not enjoined by the scriptures.
7—22	Different kinds of food, sacrifice, penance and charity described.

कृष्णात्परं किमपि तत्त्वमहं न जाने

ॐश्रीपरमात्मने नम:

The Bhagavadgītā

The Song Divine

Chapter I

धृतराष्ट्र उवाच

धर्मक्षेत्रे कुरुक्षेत्रे समवेता युयुत्सवः।
मामकाः पाण्डवाश्चैव किमकुर्वत सञ्जय॥ १॥

Dhṛtarāṣṭra said: Sañjaya, gathered on the holy land of Kurukṣetra, eager to fight, what did my sons and the sons of Pāṇḍu do? (1)

सञ्जय उवाच

दृष्ट्वा तु पाण्डवानीकं व्यूढं दुर्योधनस्तदा।
आचार्यमुपसङ्गम्य राजा वचनमब्रवीत्॥ २॥

Sañjaya said: At that time, seeing the army of the Pāṇḍavas drawn up for battle and approaching Droṇācārya, King Duryodhana spoke the following words : (2)

पश्यैतां पाण्डुपुत्राणामाचार्य महतीं चमूम्।
व्यूढां द्रुपदपुत्रेण तव शिष्येण धीमता॥ ३॥

Behold, O Revered Master, the mighty army of the sons of Pāṇḍu arrayed for battle by your talented pupil, Dhṛṣṭadyumna, son of Drupada. (3)

अत्र शूरा महेष्वासा भीमार्जुनसमा युधि।
युयुधानो विराटश्च द्रुपदश्च महारथः ॥ ४ ॥
धृष्टकेतुश्चेकितानः काशिराजश्च वीर्यवान्।
पुरुजित्कुन्तिभोजश्च शैब्यश्च नरपुङ्गवः ॥ ५ ॥
युधामन्युश्च विक्रान्त उत्तमौजाश्च वीर्यवान्।
सौभद्रो द्रौपदेयाश्च सर्व एव महारथाः ॥ ६ ॥

There are in this army, heroes wielding mighty bows and equal in military prowess to Bhīma and Arjuna—Sātyaki and Virāṭa and the Mahārathī (warrior chief) Drupada; Dhṛṣṭaketu, Cekitāna and the valiant King of Kāśī, and Purujit, Kuntibhoja, and Śaibya, the best of men, and mighty Yudhāmanyu, and valiant Uttamaujā, Abhimanyu, the son of Subhadrā, and the five sons of Draupadī—all of them Mahārathīs (warrior chiefs). (4—6)

अस्माकं तु विशिष्टा ये तान्निबोध द्विजोत्तम।
नायका मम सैन्यस्य सञ्ज्ञार्थं तान्ब्रवीमि ते ॥ ७ ॥

O best of Brāhmaṇas, know them also who are the principal warriors on our side— the generals of my army. For your information I mention them. (7)

भवान्भीष्मश्च कर्णश्च कृपश्च समितिञ्जयः।
अश्वत्थामा विकर्णश्च सौमदत्तिस्तथैव च ॥ ८ ॥

"Yourself and Bhīṣma and Karṇa and Kṛpa, who is ever victorious in battle; and even so Aśvatthāmā, Vikarṇa and Bhūriśravā (the son of Somadatta); (8)

अन्ये च बहवः शूरा मदर्थे त्यक्तजीविताः।
नानाशस्त्रप्रहरणाः सर्वे युद्धविशारदाः॥ ९ ॥

And there are many other heroes, all skilled in warfare equipped with various weapons and missiles, who have staked their lives for me.(9)

अपर्याप्तं तदस्माकं बलं भीष्माभिरक्षितम्।
पर्याप्तं त्विदमेतेषां बलं भीमाभिरक्षितम्॥ १० ॥

This army of ours, fully protected by Bhīṣma, is unconquerable; while that army of theirs, guarded in everyway by Bhīma, is easy to conquer.(10)

अयनेषु च सर्वेषु यथाभागमवस्थिताः।
भीष्ममेवाभिरक्षन्तु भवन्तः सर्व एव हि॥ ११ ॥

Therefore, stationed in your respective positions on all fronts, do you all guard Bhīṣma in particular on all sides. (11)

तस्य सञ्जनयन्हर्षं कुरुवृद्धः पितामहः।
सिंहनादं विनद्योच्चैः शङ्खं दध्मौ प्रतापवान्॥ १२ ॥

The grand old man of the Kaurava race, their glorious grand-patriarch Bhīṣma, cheering up Duryodhana, roared terribly like a lion and blew his conch. (12)

ततः शङ्खाश्च भेर्यश्च पणवानकगोमुखाः।
सहसैवाभ्यहन्यन्त स शब्दस्तुमुलोऽभवत्॥ १३ ॥

Then conches, kettledrums, tabors, drums and trumpets blared forth all at once and the noise was tumultuous. (13)

ततः श्वेतैर्हयैर्युक्ते महति स्यन्दने स्थितौ।
माधवः पाण्डवश्चैव दिव्यौ शङ्खौ प्रदध्मतुः ॥ १४ ॥

Then, seated in a glorious chariot drawn by white horses, Śrī Kṛṣṇa as well as Arjuna blew their celestial conches. (14)

पाञ्चजन्यं हृषीकेशो देवदत्तं धनञ्जयः।
पौण्ड्रं दध्मौ महाशङ्खं भीमकर्मा वृकोदरः ॥ १५ ॥

Śrī Kṛṣṇa blew His conch named Pāñcajanya; Arjuna, Devadatta; while Bhīma of ferocious deeds blew his mighty conch Pauṇḍra. (15)

अनन्तविजयं राजा कुन्तीपुत्रो युधिष्ठिरः।
नकुलः सहदेवश्च सुघोषमणिपुष्पकौ ॥ १६ ॥

King Yudhiṣṭhira, son of Kuntī, blew his conch Anantavijaya, while Nakula and Sahadeva blew theirs, known as Sughoṣa and Maṇipuṣpaka respectively. (16)

काश्यश्च परमेष्वासः शिखण्डी च महारथः।
धृष्टद्युम्नो विराटश्च सात्यकिश्चापराजितः ॥ १७ ॥
द्रुपदो द्रौपदेयाश्च सर्वशः पृथिवीपते।
सौभद्रश्च महाबाहुः शङ्खान्दध्मुः पृथक् पृथक् ॥ १८ ॥

And the excellent archer, the King of Kāśī, and Śikhaṇḍī the Mahārathī (the great chariot-warrior), Dhṛṣṭadyumna and Virāṭa, and invincible Sātyaki, Drupada as well as the five sons of Draupadī, and the mighty-armed Abhimanyu, son of Subhadrā, all of them, O lord of the earth, severally blew their respective conches from all sides. (17-18)

स घोषो धार्तराष्ट्राणां हृदयानि व्यदारयत्।
नभश्च पृथिवीं चैव तुमुलो व्यनुनादयन्॥ १९॥

And the terrible sound, echoing through heaven and earth, rent the hearts of Dhṛtarāṣṭra's army. (19)

अथ व्यवस्थितान्दृष्ट्वा धार्तराष्ट्रान् कपिध्वजः।
प्रवृत्ते शस्त्रसम्पाते धनुरुद्यम्य पाण्डवः॥ २०॥
हृषीकेशं तदा वाक्यमिदमाह महीपते।

अर्जुन उवाच

सेनयोरुभयोर्मध्ये रथं स्थापय मेऽच्युत॥ २१॥

Now, O lord of the earth, seeing your sons arrayed against him and when missiles were ready to be hurled, Arjuna, who had the figure of Hanumān on the flag of his chariot, took up his bow and then addressed the following words to Śrī Kṛṣṇa; "Kṛṣṇa, place my chariot between the two armies. (20-21)

यावदेतान्निरीक्षेऽहं योद्धुकामानवस्थितान्।
कैर्मया सह योद्धव्यमस्मिन्रणसमुद्यमे॥ २२॥

"And keep it there till I have carefully observed these warriors drawn up for battle, and have seen with whom I have to engage in this fight. (22)

योत्स्यमानानवेक्षेऽहं य एतेऽत्र समागताः।
धार्तराष्ट्रस्य दुर्बुद्धेर्युद्धे प्रियचिकीर्षवः॥ २३॥

"I shall have a look at the well-wishers of evil-minded Duryodhana, in this war whoever have assembled on his side and are ready for the fight."(23)

सञ्जय उवाच

एवमुक्तो हृषीकेशो गुडाकेशेन भारत।
सेनयोरुभयोर्मध्ये स्थापयित्वा रथोत्तमम्॥ २४॥
भीष्मद्रोणप्रमुखतः सर्वेषां च महीक्षिताम्।
उवाच पार्थ पश्यैतान्समवेतान्कुरूनिति॥ २५॥

Sañjaya said: O king, thus addressed by Arjuna, Śrī Kṛṣṇa placed the magnificent chariot between the two armies in front of Bhīṣma, Droṇa and all the kings and said, "Arjuna, behold these Kauravas assembled here." (24-25)

तत्रापश्यत्स्थितान्पार्थः पितॄनथ पितामहान्।
आचार्यान्मातुलान्भ्रातॄन्पुत्रान्पौत्रान्सखींस्तथा॥ २६॥
श्वशुरान्सुहृदश्चैव सेनयोरुभयोरपि।

Now Arjuna saw stationed there in both the armies his uncles, grand-uncles and teachers, even great grand-uncles, maternal uncles, brothers and cousins, sons and nephews, and grand-nephews, even so friends, fathers-in-law and well-wishers as well. (26 & first half of 27)

तान्समीक्ष्य स कौन्तेयः सर्वान्बन्धूनवस्थितान्॥ २७॥
कृपया परयाविष्टो विषीदन्निदमब्रवीत्।

Seeing all the relations present there, Arjuna was overcome with deep compassion and spoke thus in sorrow.

(Second half of 27 and first half of 28)

अर्जुन उवाच

दृष्ट्वेमं स्वजनं कृष्ण युयुत्सुं समुपस्थितम्॥ २८॥
सीदन्ति मम गात्राणि मुखं च परिशुष्यति।
वेपथुश्च शरीरे मे रोमहर्षश्च जायते॥ २९॥

Arjuna said: Kṛṣṇa, as I see these kinsmen arrayed for battle, my limbs give way, and my mouth is getting parched; nay, a shiver runs through my body and hair stands on end.

(Second half of 28 and 29)

गाण्डीवं स्रंसते हस्तात्त्वक्चैव परिदह्यते।
न च शक्नोम्यवस्थातुं भ्रमतीव च मे मनः॥ ३०॥

The bow, Gāṇḍīva, slips from my hand and my skin too burns all over; my mind is whirling, as it were, and I can no longer hold myself steady. (30)

निमित्तानि च पश्यामि विपरीतानि केशव।
न च श्रेयोऽनुपश्यामि हत्वा स्वजनमाहवे॥ ३१॥

And, Keśava, I see omens of evil, nor do I see any good in killing my kinsmen in battle. (31)

न काङ्क्षे विजयं कृष्ण न च राज्यं सुखानि च।
किं नो राज्येन गोविन्द किं भोगैर्जीवितेन वा॥ ३२॥

Kṛṣṇa, I do not covet victory, nor kingdom, nor pleasures. Govinda, of what use will kingdom or luxuries or even life be to us! (32)

येषामर्थे काङ्क्षितं नो राज्यं भोगाः सुखानि च।
त इमेऽवस्थिता युद्धे प्राणांस्त्यक्त्वा धनानि च॥ ३३॥
आचार्याः पितरः पुत्रास्तथैव च पितामहाः।
मातुलाः श्वशुराः पौत्राः श्यालाः सम्बन्धिनस्तथा॥ ३४॥

Those very persons for whose sake we covet the kingdom, luxuries and pleasures–teachers, uncles, sons and nephews and even so, grand-uncles and great grand-uncles, maternal uncles, fathers-in-law, grand-nephews, brothers-in-law and other relations–are here arrayed on the battlefield staking their lives and wealth. (33-34)

एतान्न हन्तुमिच्छामि घ्नतोऽपि मधुसूदन।
अपि त्रैलोक्यराज्यस्य हेतोः किं नु महीकृते॥ ३५॥

O Slayer of Madhu, I do not want to kill them, though they may slay me, even for the sovereignty over the three worlds; how much the less for the kingdom here on earth! (35)

निहत्य धार्तराष्ट्रान्नः का प्रीतिः स्याज्जनार्दन।
पापमेवाश्रयेदस्मान्हत्वैतानाततायिनः॥ ३६॥

Kṛṣṇa, how can we hope to be happy slaying the sons of Dhṛtarāṣṭra; by killing even these desperadoes, sin will surely accrue to us. (36)

तस्मान्नार्हा वयं हन्तुं धार्तराष्ट्रान्स्वबान्धवान्।
स्वजनं हि कथं हत्वा सुखिनः स्याम माधव॥ ३७॥

Therefore, Kṛṣṇa, it does not behove us to kill our relations, the sons of Dhṛtarāṣṭra. For, how can we be happy after killing our own kinsmen? (37)

यद्यप्येते न पश्यन्ति लोभोपहतचेतसः।
कुलक्षयकृतं दोषं मित्रद्रोहे च पातकम्॥ ३८॥
कथं न ज्ञेयमस्माभिः पापादस्मान्निवर्तितुम्।
कुलक्षयकृतं दोषं प्रपश्यद्भिर्जनार्दन॥ ३९॥

Even though these people, with their mind blinded by greed, perceive no evil in destroying their own race and no sin in treason to friends, why should not we, O Kṛṣṇa, who see clearly the sin accruing from the destruction of one's family, think of desisting from committing this sin. (38-39)

कुलक्षये प्रणश्यन्ति कुलधर्माः सनातनाः।
धर्मे नष्टे कुलं कृत्स्नमधर्मोऽभिभवत्युत॥ ४०॥

Age-long family traditions disappear with the destruction of a family; and virtue having been lost, vice takes hold of the entire race. (40)

अधर्माभिभवात्कृष्ण प्रदुष्यन्ति कुलस्त्रियः।
स्त्रीषु दुष्टासु वार्ष्णेय जायते वर्णसङ्करः॥ ४१॥

With the preponderance of vice, Kṛṣṇa, the women of the family become corrupt; and with the corruption of women, O descendant of Vṛṣṇi, there ensues an intermixture of castes. (41)

सङ्करो नरकायैव कुलघ्नानां कुलस्य च।
पतन्ति पितरो ह्येषां लुप्तपिण्डोदकक्रियाः॥ ४२॥

Progeny owing to promiscuity damns the destroyers of the race as well as the race itself. Deprived of the offerings of rice and water (Śrāddha, Tarpaṇa etc.,) the manes of their race also fall. (42)

दोषैरेतैः कुलघ्नानां वर्णसङ्करकारकैः।
उत्साद्यन्ते जातिधर्माः कुलधर्माश्च शाश्वताः॥ ४३॥

Through these evils bringing about an intermixture of castes, the age-long caste traditions and family customs of the killers of kinsmen get extinct. (43)

उत्सन्नकुलधर्माणां मनुष्याणां जनार्दन।
नरकेऽनियतं वासो भवतीत्यनुशुश्रुम॥ ४४॥

Kṛṣṇa, we hear that men who have lost their family traditions, dwell in hell for an indefinite period of time. (44)

अहो बत महत्पापं कर्तुं व्यवसिता वयम्।
यद्राज्यसुखलोभेन हन्तुं स्वजनमुद्यताः॥ ४५॥

Oh what a pity! Though possessed of intelligence we have set our mind on the commission of a great sin; that due to lust for throne and enjoyment we are intent on killing our own kinsmen. (45)

यदि मामप्रतीकारमशस्त्रं शस्त्रपाणयः।
धार्तराष्ट्रा रणे हन्युस्तन्मे क्षेमतरं भवेत्॥ ४६॥

It would be better for me if the sons of Dhṛtarāṣṭra, armed with weapons, kill me in battle, while I am unarmed and unresisting. (46)

सञ्जय उवाच

एवमुक्त्वार्जुनः सङ्ख्ये रथोपस्थ उपाविशत्।
विसृज्य सशरं चापं शोकसंविग्नमानसः ॥ ४७ ॥

Sañjaya said: Arjuna, whose mind was agitated by grief on the battlefield, having spoken thus, and having cast aside his bow and arrows, sank into the hinder part of his chariot. (47)

ॐ तत्सदिति श्रीमद्भगवद्गीतासूपनिषत्सु ब्रह्मविद्यायां योगशास्त्रे श्रीकृष्णार्जुनसंवादेऽर्जुनविषादयोगो नाम प्रथमोऽध्यायः ॥ १ ॥

Thus, in the Upaniṣad sung by the Lord, the Science of Brahma, the scripture of Yoga, the dialogue between Śrī Kṛṣṇa and Arjuna, ends the first chapter entitled "The Yoga of Dejection of Arjuna."

Chapter II

सञ्जय उवाच

तं तथा कृपयाविष्टमश्रुपूर्णाकुलेक्षणम्।
विषीदन्तमिदं वाक्यमुवाच मधुसूदनः॥ १॥

Sañjaya said : Śrī Kṛṣṇa then addressed the following words to Arjuna, who was, as mentioned before, overwhelmed with pity, whose eyes were filled with tears and agitated, and who was full of sorrow. (1)

श्रीभगवानुवाच

कुतस्त्वा कश्मलमिदं विषमे समुपस्थितम्।
अनार्यजुष्टमस्वर्ग्यमकीर्तिकरमर्जुन ॥ २॥

Śrī Bhagavān said : Arjuna, how has this infatuation overtaken you at this odd hour? It is shunned by noble souls; neither will it bring heaven, nor fame to you. (2)

क्लैब्यं मा स्म गमः पार्थ नैतत्त्वय्युपपद्यते।
क्षुद्रं हृदयदौर्बल्यं त्यक्त्वोत्तिष्ठ परन्तप॥ ३॥

Yield not to unmanliness, Arjuna; this does not become you. Shaking off this base faint-heartedness stand-up, O scorcher of enemies.(3)

अर्जुन उवाच

कथं भीष्ममहं सङ्ख्ये द्रोणं च मधुसूदन।
इषुभिः प्रतियोत्स्यामि पूजार्हावरिसूदन॥ ४॥

Arjuna said : How Kṛṣṇa, shall I fight Bhīṣma and Droṇa with arrows on the battlefield? They are worthy of deepest reverence, O destroyer of foes. (4)

गुरूनहत्वा हि महानुभावान्
श्रेयो भोक्तुं भैक्ष्यमपीह लोके।
हत्वार्थकामांस्तु गुरूनिहैव
भुञ्जीय भोगान् रुधिरप्रदिग्धान्॥ ५ ॥

It is better to live on alms in this world by not slaying these noble elders, because even after killing them we shall after all enjoy only bloodstained pleasures in the form of wealth and sense-enjoyments. (5)

न चैतद्विद्मः कतरन्नो गरीयो-
यद्वा जयेम यदि वा नो जयेयुः।
यानेव हत्वा न जिजीविषाम-
स्तेऽवस्थिताः प्रमुखे धार्तराष्ट्राः ॥ ६ ॥

We do not even know which is preferable for us—to fight or not to fight; nor do we know whether we shall win or whether they will conquer us. Those very sons of Dhṛtarāṣṭra, killing whom we do not even wish to live, stand in the enemy ranks. (6)

कार्पण्यदोषोपहतस्वभावः
पृच्छामि त्वां धर्मसम्मूढचेताः।
यच्छ्रेयः स्यान्निश्चितं ब्रूहि तन्मे
शिष्यस्तेऽहं शाधि मां त्वां प्रपन्नम्॥ ७ ॥

With my very being smitten by the vice of faint-heartedness and my mind puzzled with regard to duty, I beseech You! tell me that which is decidedly good; I am your disciple. Pray, instruct me, who have taken refuge in You. (7)

न हि प्रपश्यामि ममापनुद्याद्
यच्छोकमुच्छोषणमिन्द्रियाणाम् ।
अवाप्य भूमावसपत्नमृद्धं-
राज्यं सुराणामपि चाधिपत्यम् ॥ ८ ॥

For, even on obtaining undisputed sovereignty and an affluent kingdom on this earth and lordship over the gods, I do not see any means that can drive away the grief which is drying up my senses. (8)

सञ्जय उवाच

एवमुक्त्वा हृषीकेशं गुडाकेशः परन्तप।
न योत्स्य इति गोविन्दमुक्त्वा तूष्णीं बभूव ह॥ ९ ॥

Sañjaya said : O King, having thus spoken to Śrī Kṛṣṇa, Arjuna again said to Him, "I will not fight," and became silent. (9)

तमुवाच हृषीकेशः प्रहसन्निव भारत।
सेनयोरुभयोर्मध्ये विषीदन्तमिदं वचः॥ १० ॥

Then, O Dhṛtarāṣṭra, Śrī Kṛṣṇa, as if smiling, addressed the following words to Arjuna, sorrowing in the midst of the two armies. (10)

श्रीभगवानुवाच

अशोच्यानन्वशोचस्त्वं प्रज्ञावादांश्च भाषसे।
गतासूनगतासूंश्च नानुशोचन्ति पण्डिताः ॥ ११ ॥

Śrī Bhagavān said: Arjuna, you grieve over those who should not be grieved for and yet speak like the learned; wise men do not sorrow over the dead or the living. (11)

न त्वेवाहं जातु नासं न त्वं नेमे जनाधिपाः।
न चैव न भविष्यामः सर्वे वयमतः परम् ॥ १२ ॥

In fact, there was never a time when I was not, or when you or these kings were not. Nor is it a fact that hereafter we shall all cease to be. (12)

देहिनोऽस्मिन्यथा देहे कौमारं यौवनं जरा।
तथा देहान्तरप्राप्तिर्धीरस्तत्र न मुह्यति ॥ १३ ॥

Just as boyhood, youth and old age are attributed to the soul through this body, even so it attains another body. The wise man does not get deluded about this. (13)

मात्रास्पर्शास्तु कौन्तेय शीतोष्णसुखदुःखदाः।
आगमापायिनोऽनित्यास्तांस्तितिक्षस्व भारत ॥ १४ ॥

O son of Kuntī, the contacts between the senses and their objects, which give rise to the feelings of heat and cold, pleasure and pain etc., are transitory and fleeting; therefore, Arjuna, endure them. (14)

यं हि न व्यथयन्त्येते पुरुषं पुरुषर्षभ।
समदुःखसुखं धीरं सोऽमृतत्वाय कल्पते ॥ १५ ॥

Arjuna, the wise man to whom pain and pleasure are alike, and who is not tormented by these contacts, becomes eligible for immortality. (15)

नासतो विद्यते भावो नाभावो विद्यते सतः।
उभयोरपि दृष्टोऽन्तस्त्वनयोस्तत्त्वदर्शिभिः॥ १६॥

The unreal has no existence, and the real never ceases to be; the reality of both has thus been perceived by the seers of Truth. (16)

अविनाशि तु तद्विद्धि येन सर्वमिदं ततम्।
विनाशमव्ययस्यास्य न कश्चित्कर्तुमर्हति॥ १७॥

Know that alone to be imperishable which pervades this universe; for no one has power to destroy this indestructible substance. (17)

अन्तवन्त इमे देहा नित्यस्योक्ताः शरीरिणः।
अनाशिनोऽप्रमेयस्य तस्माद्युध्यस्व भारत॥ १८॥

All these bodies pertaining to the imperishable, indefinable and eternal soul are spoken of as perishable; therefore, Arjuna, fight. (18)

य एनं वेत्ति हन्तारं यश्चैनं मन्यते हतम्।
उभौ तौ न विजानीतो नायं हन्ति न हन्यते॥ १९॥

Both of them are ignorant, he who considers the soul to be capable of killing and he who takes it as killed; for verily the soul neither kills, nor is killed. (19)

न जायते म्रियते वा कदाचि-
न्नायं भूत्वा भविता वा न भूयः।
अजो नित्यः शाश्वतोऽयं पुराणो-
न हन्यते हन्यमाने शरीरे॥ २०॥

The soul is never born, nor it ever dies; nor does it become after being born. For, it is unborn, eternal, everlasting and primeval; even though the body is slain, the soul is not. (20)

वेदाविनाशिनं नित्यं य एनमजमव्ययम्।
कथं स पुरुषः पार्थ कं घातयति हन्ति कम्॥ २१॥

Arjuna, the man who knows this soul to be imperishable; eternal and free from birth and decay—how and whom will he cause to be killed, how and whom will he kill? (21)

वासांसि जीर्णानि यथा विहाय
नवानि गृह्णाति नरोऽपराणि।
तथा शरीराणि विहाय जीर्णा-
न्यन्यानि संयाति नवानि देही॥ २२॥

As a man shedding worn-out garments, takes other new ones, likewise, the embodied soul, casting off worn-out bodies, enters into others that are new. (22)

नैनं छिन्दन्ति शस्त्राणि नैनं दहति पावकः।
न चैनं क्लेदयन्त्यापो न शोषयति मारुतः॥ २३॥

Weapons cannot cut it nor can fire burn it; water cannot wet it nor can wind dry it. (23)

अच्छेद्योऽयमदाह्योऽयमक्लेद्योऽशोष्य एव च।
नित्यः सर्वगतः स्थाणुरचलोऽयं सनातनः॥ २४॥

For this soul is incapable of being cut, or burnt by fire; nor can it be dissolved by water and is undriable by air as well; This soul is eternal, all-pervading, immovable, constant and everlasting. (24)

अव्यक्तोऽयमचिन्त्योऽयमविकार्योऽयमुच्यते ।
तस्मादेवं विदित्वैनं नानुशोचितुमर्हसि ॥ २५ ॥

This soul is unmanifest; it is incomprehensible and it is spoken of as immutable. Therefore, knowing it as such, you should not grieve. (25)

अथ चैनं नित्यजातं नित्यं वा मन्यसे मृतम् ।
तथापि त्वं महाबाहो नैवं शोचितुमर्हसि ॥ २६ ॥

And, Arjuna, if you should suppose this soul to be subject to constant birth and death, even then you should not grieve like this. (26)

जातस्य हि ध्रुवो मृत्युर्ध्रुवं जन्म मृतस्य च ।
तस्मादपरिहार्येऽर्थे न त्वं शोचितुमर्हसि ॥ २७ ॥

For, in that case death is certain for the born, and rebirth is inevitable for the dead. You should not, therefore, grieve over the inevitable. (27)

अव्यक्तादीनि भूतानि व्यक्तमध्यानि भारत ।
अव्यक्तनिधनान्येव तत्र का परिदेवना ॥ २८ ॥

Arjuna, before birth beings are not manifest to our human senses; on death they return to the unmanifest again. They are manifest only in the interim between birth and death. What occasion, then, for lamentation? (28)

आश्चर्यवत्पश्यति कश्चिदेन-
माश्चर्यवद्वदति तथैव चान्यः ।
आश्चर्यवच्चैनमन्यः शृणोति
श्रुत्वाप्येनं वेद न चैव कश्चित् ॥ २९ ॥

Hardly any great soul perceives this soul as marvellous, scarce another great soul likewise speaks thereof as marvellous, and scarce another worthy one hears of it as marvellous, while there are some who know it not even on hearing of it.(29)

देही नित्यमवध्योऽयं देहे सर्वस्य भारत।
तस्मात्सर्वाणि भूतानि न त्वं शोचितुमर्हसि॥ ३०॥

Arjuna, this soul dwelling in the bodies of all, can never be slain; therefore, you should not mourn for anyone. (30)

स्वधर्ममपि चावेक्ष्य न विकम्पितुमर्हसि।
धर्म्याद्धि युद्धाच्छ्रेयोऽन्यत्क्षत्रियस्य न विद्यते॥ ३१॥

Besides, considering your own duty too, you should not waver, for there is nothing more welcome for a man of the warrior class than a righteous war. (31)

यदृच्छया चोपपन्नं स्वर्गद्वारमपावृतम्।
सुखिनः क्षत्रियाः पार्थ लभन्ते युद्धमीदृशम्॥ ३२॥

Arjuna, fortunate are the Kṣatriyas who get such an unsolicited opportunity for war, which is an open gateway to heaven. (32)

अथ चेत्त्वमिमं धर्म्यं सङ्ग्रामं न करिष्यसि।
ततः स्वधर्मं कीर्तिं च हित्वा पापमवाप्स्यसि॥ ३३॥

Now, if you refuse to fight this righteous war, then, shirking your duty and losing your reputation, you will incur sin. (33)

अकीर्तिं चापि भूतानि कथयिष्यन्ति तेऽव्ययाम्।
सम्भावितस्य चाकीर्तिर्मरणादतिरिच्यते॥ ३४॥

Nay, people will also pour undying infamy on you; and infamy brought on a man enjoying popular esteem is worse than death. (34)

भयाद्रणादुपरतं मंस्यन्ते त्वां महारथाः।
येषां च त्वं बहुमतो भूत्वा यास्यसि लाघवम्॥ ३५॥

And the warrior-chiefs who thought highly of you, will now despise you, thinking that it was fear which drove you away from battle. (35)

अवाच्यवादांश्च बहून्वदिष्यन्ति तवाहिताः।
निन्दन्तस्तव सामर्थ्यं ततो दुःखतरं नु किम्॥ ३६॥

And your enemies, disparaging your might, will speak many unbecoming words; what can be more distressing than this? (36)

हतो वा प्राप्स्यसि स्वर्गं जित्वा वा भोक्ष्यसे महीम्।
तस्मादुत्तिष्ठ कौन्तेय युद्धाय कृतनिश्चयः॥ ३७॥

Die, and you will win heaven; conquer, and you enjoy sovereignty of the earth; therefore, stand up, Arjuna, determined to fight. (37)

सुखदुःखे समे कृत्वा लाभालाभौ जयाजयौ।
ततो युद्धाय युज्यस्व नैवं पापमवाप्स्यसि॥ ३८॥

Treating alike victory and defeat, gain and loss, pleasure and pain, get ready for the battle; fighting thus you will not incur sin. (38)

एषा तेऽभिहिता साङ्ख्ये बुद्धिर्योगे त्विमां शृणु।
बुद्ध्या युक्तो यया पार्थ कर्मबन्धं प्रहास्यसि॥ ३९॥

Arjuna, this attitude of mind has been presented

to you from the point of view of Jñānayoga; now hear the same as presented from the standpoint of Karmayoga (the Yoga of selfless action). Equipped with this attitude of mind, you will be able to throw off completely the shackles of Karma. (39)

नेहाभिक्रमनाशोऽस्ति प्रत्यवायो न विद्यते।
स्वल्पमप्यस्य धर्मस्य त्रायते महतो भयात्॥ ४०॥

In this path (of selfless action) there is no loss of effort, nor is there fear of contrary result, even a little practice of this discipline saves one from the terrible fear of birth and death. (40)

व्यवसायात्मिका बुद्धिरेकेह कुरुनन्दन।
बहुशाखा ह्यनन्ताश्च बुद्धयोऽव्यवसायिनाम्॥ ४१॥

Arjuna, in this Yoga (of selfless action) the intellect is determinate and directed singly towards one ideal; whereas the intellect of the undecided (ignorant men moved by desires) wanders in all directions after innumerable aims. (41)

यामिमां पुष्पितां वाचं प्रवदन्त्यविपश्चितः।
वेदवादरताः पार्थ नान्यदस्तीति वादिनः॥ ४२॥
कामात्मानः स्वर्गपरा जन्मकर्मफलप्रदाम्।
क्रियाविशेषबहुलां भोगैश्वर्यगतिं प्रति॥ ४३॥
भोगैश्वर्यप्रसक्तानां तयापहृतचेतसाम्।
व्यवसायात्मिका बुद्धिः समाधौ न विधीयते॥ ४४॥

Arjuna, those who are full of worldly desires and devoted to the letter of the Vedas, who look upon heaven as the supreme goal and argue that there is nothing beyond heaven, are unwise. They utter flowery speech recommending many rituals of various kinds for the attainment of pleasure and power with rebirth as their fruit. Those whose minds are carried away by such words, and who are deeply attached to pleasures and worldly power, cannot attain the determinate intellect concentrated on God. (42—44)

त्रैगुण्यविषया वेदा निस्त्रैगुण्यो भवार्जुन।
निर्द्वन्द्वो नित्यसत्त्वस्थो निर्योगक्षेम आत्मवान्॥ ४५॥

Arjuna, the Vedas thus deal with the evolutes of the three Guṇas (modes of Prakṛti), viz., worldly enjoyments and the means of attaining such enjoyments; be thou indifferent to these enjoyments and their means, rising above pairs of opposites like pleasure and pain etc., established in the Eternal Existence (God), absolutely unconcerned about the fulfilment of wants and the preservation of what has been already attained, you be self-controlled.(45)

यावानर्थ उदपाने सर्वतः सम्प्लुतोदके।
तावान्सर्वेषु वेदेषु ब्राह्मणस्य विजानतः॥ ४६॥

A Brāhmaṇa, who has obtained enlightenment, has as much use for all the Vedas as one who stands at the brink of a sheet of water overflowing on all sides has for a small reservoir of water. (46)

कर्मण्येवाधिकारस्ते मा फलेषु कदाचन।
मा कर्मफलहेतुर्भूर्मा ते सङ्गोऽस्त्वकर्मणि॥ ४७॥

Your right is to work only and never to the fruit thereof. Do not Consider yourself to be the cause of the fruit of action; nor let your attachment be to inaction. (47)

योगस्थः कुरु कर्माणि सङ्गं त्यक्त्वा धनञ्जय।
सिद्ध्यसिद्ध्योः समो भूत्वा समत्वं योग उच्यते॥ ४८॥

Arjuna, perform your duties established in Yoga, renouncing attachment, and be even-minded in success and failure; evenness of mind is called 'Yoga'. (48)

दूरेण ह्यवरं कर्म बुद्धियोगाद्धनञ्जय।
बुद्धौ शरणमन्विच्छ कृपणाः फलहेतवः॥ ४९॥

Action with a selfish motive is far inferior to this Yoga in the form of equanimity. Do seek refuge in this equipoise of mind, Arjuna; for poor and wretched are those who are the cause in making their actions bear fruit. (49)

बुद्धियुक्तो जहातीह उभे सुकृतदुष्कृते।
तस्माद्योगाय युज्यस्व योगः कर्मसु कौशलम्॥ ५०॥

Endowed with equanimity, one sheds in this life both good and evil. Therefore, strive for the practice of this Yoga of equanimity. Skill in action lies in the practice of this Yoga. (50)

कर्मजं बुद्धियुक्ता हि फलं त्यक्त्वा मनीषिणः।
जन्मबन्धविनिर्मुक्ताः पदं गच्छन्त्यनामयम्॥ ५१॥

For, wise men possessing equipoised mind, renouncing the fruit of actions and freed from the shackles of birth, attain the blissful supreme state. (51)

यदा ते मोहकलिलं बुद्धिर्व्यतितरिष्यति।
तदा गन्तासि निर्वेदं श्रोतव्यस्य श्रुतस्य च॥ ५२॥

When your mind will have fully crossed the mire of delusion, you will then grow indifferent to the enjoyments of this world and the next that have been heard of as well as to those that are yet to be heard of. (52)

श्रुतिविप्रतिपन्ना ते यदा स्थास्यति निश्चला।
समाधावचला बुद्धिस्तदा योगमवाप्स्यसि॥ ५३॥

When your intellect, confused by hearing conflicting statements, will rest steady and undistracted (in meditation) on God, you will then attain Yoga (everlasting union with God). (53)

अर्जुन उवाच

स्थितप्रज्ञस्य का भाषा समाधिस्थस्य केशव।
स्थितधीः किं प्रभाषेत किमासीत व्रजेत किम्॥ ५४॥

Arjuna said : Kṛṣṇa, what are the characteristics of a God-realized soul, stable of mind and established in Samādhi (perfect tranquillity of mind)? How does the man of stable mind speak, how does he sit, how does he walk? (54)

श्रीभगवानुवाच

प्रजहाति यदा कामान्सर्वान्पार्थ मनोगतान्।
आत्मन्येवात्मना तुष्टः स्थितप्रज्ञस्तदोच्यते॥ ५५॥

Śrī Bhagavān said: Arjuna, when one thoroughly casts off all cravings of the mind, and is satisfied in the Self through the joy of the Self, he is then called stable of mind. (55)

दुःखेष्वनुद्विग्नमनाः सुखेषु विगतस्पृहः।
वीतरागभयक्रोधः स्थितधीर्मुनिरुच्यते॥ ५६॥

The sage, whose mind remains unperturbed amid sorrows, whose thirst for pleasures has altogether disappeared, and who is free from passion, fear and anger, is called stable of mind. (56)

यः सर्वत्रानभिस्नेहस्तत्तत्प्राप्य शुभाशुभम्।
नाभिनन्दति न द्वेष्टि तस्य प्रज्ञा प्रतिष्ठिता॥ ५७॥

He who is unattached to everything, and meeting with good and evil, neither rejoices nor recoils, his mind is stable. (57)

यदा संहरते चायं कूर्मोऽङ्गानीव सर्वशः।
इन्द्रियाणीन्द्रियार्थेभ्यस्तस्य प्रज्ञा प्रतिष्ठिता॥ ५८॥

When, like a tortoise, that draws in its limbs from all directions, he withdraws all his senses from the sense-objects, his mind becomes steady. (58)

विषया विनिवर्तन्ते निराहारस्य देहिनः।
रसवर्जं रसोऽप्यस्य परं दृष्ट्वा निवर्तते॥ ५९॥

Sense-objects turn away from him, who does not enjoy them with his senses; but the taste for them persists. This relish also disappears in the case of the man of stable mind when he realizes the Supreme. (59)

यततो ह्यपि कौन्तेय पुरुषस्य विपश्चितः।
इन्द्रियाणि प्रमाथीनि हरन्ति प्रसभं मनः॥ ६०॥

Turbulent by nature, the senses (not free from attachment) even of a wise man, who is practising self-control, forcibly carry away his mind, Arjuna.(60)

तानि सर्वाणि संयम्य युक्त आसीत मत्परः।
वशे हि यस्येन्द्रियाणि तस्य प्रज्ञा प्रतिष्ठिता॥ ६१॥

Therefore, having controlled all the senses and concentrating his mind, he should sit for meditation, devoting himself heart and soul to Me.

For, he whose senses are under his control, is known to have a stable mind. (61)

ध्यायतो विषयान्पुंसः सङ्गस्तेषूपजायते।
सङ्गात्सञ्जायते कामः कामात्क्रोधोऽभिजायते॥ ६२॥

The man dwelling on sense-objects develops attachment for them; from attachment springs up desire, and from desire (unfulfilled) ensues anger. (62)

क्रोधाद्भवति सम्मोहः सम्मोहात्स्मृतिविभ्रमः।
स्मृतिभ्रंशाद् बुद्धिनाशो बुद्धिनाशात्प्रणश्यति॥ ६३॥

From anger arises delusion; from delusion, confusion of memory; from confusion of memory, loss of reason; and from loss of reason one goes to complete ruin. (63)

रागद्वेषवियुक्तैस्तु विषयानिन्द्रियैश्चरन्।
आत्मवश्यैर्विधेयात्मा प्रसादमधिगच्छति॥ ६४॥

But the self-controlled Sādhaka, while enjoying the various sense-objects through his senses, which are disciplined and free from likes and dislikes, attains placidity of mind. (64)

प्रसादे सर्वदुःखानां हानिरस्योपजायते।
प्रसन्नचेतसो ह्याशु बुद्धिः पर्यवतिष्ठते॥ ६५॥

With the attainment of such placidity of mind, all his sorrows come to an end; and the intellect of such a person of tranquil mind soon withdrawing itself from all sides, becomes firmly established in God. (65)

नास्ति बुद्धिरयुक्तस्य न चायुक्तस्य भावना।
न चाभावयतः शान्तिरशान्तस्य कुतः सुखम्॥ ६६॥

He who has not controlled his mind and senses, can have no determinate intellect, nor contemplation. Without contemplation, he can have no peace; and how can there be happiness for one lacking peace of mind? (66)

इन्द्रियाणां हि चरतां यन्मनोऽनुविधीयते।
तदस्य हरति प्रज्ञां वायुर्नावमिवाम्भसि॥ ६७॥

As the wind carries away a boat upon the waters, even so, of the senses moving among sense-objects, the one to which the mind is attached, takes away his discrimination. (67)

तस्माद्यस्य महाबाहो निगृहीतानि सर्वशः।
इन्द्रियाणीन्द्रियार्थेभ्यस्तस्य प्रज्ञा प्रतिष्ठिता॥ ६८॥

Therefore, Arjuna, he whose senses are completely restrained from their objects, is said to have a stable mind. (68)

या निशा सर्वभूतानां तस्यां जागर्ति संयमी।
यस्यां जाग्रति भूतानि सा निशा पश्यतो मुनेः॥ ६९॥

That which is night to all beings, in that state of Divine Knowledge and Supreme Bliss the God-realized Yogī keeps awake, and that (the ever-changing, transient worldly happiness) in which all beings keep awake, is night to the seer. (69)

आपूर्यमाणमचलप्रतिष्ठं-
समुद्रमापः प्रविशन्ति यद्वत्।
तद्वत्कामा यं प्रविशन्ति सर्वे
स शान्तिमाप्नोति न कामकामी॥ ७०॥

As the waters of different rivers enter the ocean, which, though full on all sides, remains undisturbed; likewise, he in whom all enjoyments merge themselves without causing disturbance attains peace; not he who hankers after such enjoyments. (70)

विहाय कामान्यः सर्वान्पुमांश्चरति निःस्पृहः।
निर्ममो निरहङ्कारः स शान्तिमधिगच्छति ॥ ७१ ॥

He who has given up all desires, and moves free from attachment, egoism and thirst for enjoyment attains peace. (71)

एषा ब्राह्मी स्थितिः पार्थ नैनां प्राप्य विमुह्यति।
स्थित्वास्यामन्तकालेऽपि ब्रह्मनिर्वाणमृच्छति ॥ ७२ ॥

Arjuna, such is the state of the God-realized soul; having reached this state, he overcomes delusion. And established in this state, even at the last moment, he attains Brahmic Bliss. (72)

ॐ तत्सदिति श्रीमद्भगवद्गीतासूपनिषत्सु ब्रह्मविद्यायां
योगशास्त्रे श्रीकृष्णार्जुनसंवादे साङ्ख्ययोगो
नाम द्वितीयोऽध्यायः ॥ २ ॥

Thus, in the Upaniṣad sung by the Lord, the Science of Brahma, the scripture of Yoga, the dialogue between Śrī Kṛṣṇa and Arjuna, ends the second chapter entitled "Sāṅkhyayoga" (the Yoga of Knowledge).

Chapter III

अर्जुन उवाच

ज्यायसी चेत्कर्मणस्ते मता बुद्धिर्जनार्दन।
तत्किं कर्मणि घोरे मां नियोजयसि केशव॥ १॥

Arjuna said : Kṛṣṇa, if You consider Knowledge as superior to Action, why then do You urge me to this dreadful action, Keśava! (1)

व्यामिश्रेणेव वाक्येन बुद्धिं मोहयसीव मे।
तदेकं वद निश्चित्य येन श्रेयोऽहमाप्नुयाम्॥ २॥

You are, as it were, puzzling my mind by these seemingly conflicting expressions; therefore, tell me the one definite discipline by which I may obtain the highest good. (2)

श्रीभगवानुवाच

लोकेऽस्मिन्द्विविधा निष्ठा पुरा प्रोक्ता मयानघ।
ज्ञानयोगेन साङ्ख्यानां कर्मयोगेन योगिनाम्॥ ३॥

Śrī Bhagavān said: Arjuna, in this world two courses of Sādhanā (spiritual discipline) have been enunciated by Me in the past. In the case of the Sāṅkhyayogī, the Sādhanā proceeds along the path of Knowledge; whereas in the case of the Karmayogī, it proceeds along the path of Action. (3)

न कर्मणामनारम्भान्नैष्कर्म्यं पुरुषोऽश्नुते।
न च सन्न्यसनादेव सिद्धिं समधिगच्छति॥ ४॥

Man does not attain freedom from action (culmination of the discipline of Action) without entering upon action; nor does he reach perfection (culmination of the discipline of Knowledge) merely by ceasing to act. (4)

न हि कश्चित्क्षणमपि जातु तिष्ठत्यकर्मकृत्।
कार्यते ह्यवशः कर्म सर्वः प्रकृतिजैर्गुणैः ॥ ५ ॥

Surely, none can ever remain inactive even for a moment; for, everyone is helplessly driven to action by modes of Prakṛti (nature born qualities). (5)

कर्मेन्द्रियाणि संयम्य य आस्ते मनसा स्मरन्।
इन्द्रियार्थान्विमूढात्मा मिथ्याचारः स उच्यते ॥ ६ ॥

He who outwardly restraining the organs of sense and action, sits mentally dwelling on the objects of senses, that man of deluded intellect is called a hypocrite. (6)

यस्त्विन्द्रियाणि मनसा नियम्यारभतेऽर्जुन।
कर्मेन्द्रियैः कर्मयोगमसक्तः स विशिष्यते ॥ ७ ॥

On the other hand, he who controlling the organs of sense and action by the power of his will, and remaining unattached, undertakes the Yoga of selfless Action through those organs, Arjuna, he excels. (7)

नियतं कुरु कर्म त्वं कर्म ज्यायो ह्यकर्मणः।
शरीरयात्रापि च ते न प्रसिद्ध्येदकर्मणः ॥ ८ ॥

Therefore, do you perform your allotted duty; for action is superior to inaction. Desisting from action, you cannot even maintain your body. (8)

यज्ञार्थात्कर्मणोऽन्यत्र लोकोऽयं कर्मबन्धनः।
तदर्थं कर्म कौन्तेय मुक्तसङ्गः समाचर॥ ९॥

Man is bound by his own action except when it is performed for the sake of sacrifice. Therefore, Arjuna, do you efficiently perform your duty, free from attachment, for the sake of sacrifice alone. (9)

सहयज्ञाः प्रजाः सृष्ट्वा पुरोवाच प्रजापतिः।
अनेन प्रसविष्यध्वमेष वोऽस्त्विष्टकामधुक्॥ १०॥

Having created mankind along with Yajña, at the beginning of creation, the creator, Brahmā, said to them, "You shall prosper by this; may this yield the enjoyments you seek. (10)

देवान्भावयतानेन ते देवा भावयन्तु वः।
परस्परं भावयन्तः श्रेयः परमवाप्स्यथ॥ ११॥

Foster the gods through this sacrifice, and let the gods foster you. Thus, each fostering the other selflessly, you will attain the highest good.(11)

इष्टान्भोगान्हि वो देवा दास्यन्ते यज्ञभाविताः।
तैर्दत्तानप्रदायैभ्यो यो भुङ्क्ते स्तेन एव सः॥ १२॥

Fostered by sacrifice, the gods will surely bestow on you unasked all the desired enjoyments. He who enjoys the gifts bestowed by them without offering their share to them, is undoubtedly a thief. (12)

यज्ञशिष्टाशिनः सन्तो मुच्यन्ते सर्वकिल्बिषैः।
भुञ्जते ते त्वघं पापा ये पचन्त्यात्मकारणात्॥ १३॥

The virtuous who partake of what is left over after sacrifice, are absolved of all sins. Those sinful ones who cook for the sake of nourishing their bodies alone, partake of sin only. (13)

अन्नाद्भवन्ति भूतानि पर्जन्यादन्नसम्भवः।
यज्ञाद्भवति पर्जन्यो यज्ञः कर्मसमुद्भवः॥ १४॥
कर्म ब्रह्मोद्भवं विद्धि ब्रह्माक्षरसमुद्भवम्।
तस्मात्सर्वगतं ब्रह्म नित्यं यज्ञे प्रतिष्ठितम्॥ १५॥

All beings are evolved from food; production of food is dependent on rain; rain ensues from sacrifice, and sacrifice is rooted in prescribed action. Know that prescribed action has its origin in the Vedas, and the Vedas proceed from the Indestructible (God); hence the all-pervading Infinite is always present in sacrifice. (14-15)

एवं प्रवर्तितं चक्रं नानुवर्तयतीह यः।
अघायुरिन्द्रियारामो मोघं पार्थ स जीवति॥ १६॥

Arjuna, he who does not follow the wheel of creation thus set going in this world i.e., does not perform his duties, leads a sinful and sensual life, he lives in vain. (16)

यस्त्वात्मरतिरेव स्यादात्मतृप्तश्च मानवः।
आत्मन्येव च सन्तुष्टस्तस्य कार्यं न विद्यते॥ १७॥

He, however, who takes delight in the Self alone and is gratified with the Self, and is contented in the Self, has no duty. (17)

नैव तस्य कृतेनार्थो नाकृतेनेह कश्चन।
न चास्य सर्वभूतेषु कश्चिदर्थव्यपाश्रयः॥ १८॥

In this world that great soul has nothing to gain by action nor by abstaining from action; nor has he selfish dependence of any kind on any creature. (18)

तस्मादसक्तः सततं कार्यं कर्म समाचर।
असक्तो ह्याचरन्कर्म परमाप्नोति पूरुषः॥ १९॥

Therefore, go on efficiently doing your duty at all times without attachment. Doing work without attachment man attains the Supreme. (19)

कर्मणैव हि संसिद्धिमास्थिता जनकादयः।
लोकसङ्ग्रहमेवापि सम्पश्यन्कर्तुमर्हसि॥ २०॥

It is through action without attachment alone that Janaka and other wise men reached perfection. Having in view the maintenance of the world order too, you should take to action. (20)

यद्यदाचरति श्रेष्ठस्तत्तदेवेतरो जनः।
स यत्प्रमाणं कुरुते लोकस्तदनुवर्तते॥ २१॥

For, whatever a great man does, that very thing other men also do; whatever standard he sets up, the generality of men follow the same. (21)

न मे पार्थास्ति कर्तव्यं त्रिषु लोकेषु किञ्चन।
नानवाप्तमवाप्तव्यं वर्त एव च कर्मणि॥ २२॥

Arjuna, there is no duty in all the three worlds for Me to perform, nor is there anything worth attaining, unattained by Me; yet I continue to work. (22)

यदि ह्यहं न वर्तेयं जातु कर्मण्यतन्द्रितः।
मम वर्त्मानुवर्तन्ते मनुष्याः पार्थ सर्वशः॥ २३॥

Should I not engage in action scrupulously at any time, great harm will come to the world; for, Arjuna, men follow My way in all matters. (23)

उत्सीदेयुरिमे लोका न कुर्यां कर्म चेदहम्।
सङ्करस्य च कर्ता स्यामुपहन्यामिमाः प्रजाः॥ २४॥

If I ever cease to act, these worlds would perish; nay, I should prove to be the cause of confusion, and of the destruction of these people. (24)

सक्ताः कर्मण्यविद्वांसो यथा कुर्वन्ति भारत।
कुर्याद्विद्वांस्तथासक्तश्चिकीर्षुर्लोकसङ्ग्रहम्॥ २५॥

Arjuna, as the unwise act with attachment, so should the wise man, with a view to maintain the world order, act without attachment. (25)

न बुद्धिभेदं जनयेदज्ञानां कर्मसङ्गिनाम्।
जोषयेत्सर्वकर्माणि विद्वान्युक्तः समाचरन्॥ २६॥

A wise man established in the Self should not unsettle the mind of the ignorant attached to action, but should get them to perform all their duties, duly performing his own duties. (26)

प्रकृतेः क्रियमाणानि गुणैः कर्माणि सर्वशः।
अहङ्कारविमूढात्मा कर्ताहमिति मन्यते॥ २७॥

In fact all actions are being performed by the modes of Prakṛti (Primordial Nature). The fool, whose mind is deluded by egoism, thinks: "I am the doer." (27)

तत्त्ववित्तु महाबाहो गुणकर्मविभागयोः।
गुणा गुणेषु वर्तन्त इति मत्वा न सज्जते॥ २८॥

However, he who has true insight into the respective spheres of Guṇas (modes of Prakṛti) and their actions, holding that it is the Guṇas (in the form of the senses, mind, etc.,) that move among the Guṇas (objects of perception), does not get attached to them, Arjuna. (28)

प्रकृतेर्गुणसम्मूढाः सज्जन्ते गुणकर्मसु।
तानकृत्स्नविदो मन्दान्कृत्स्नविन्न विचालयेत्॥ २९॥

Those who are completely deluded by the Guṇas (modes) of Prakṛti remain attached to those Guṇas and actions; the man of perfect Knowledge should not unsettle the mind of those ignorants of imperfect knowledge. (29)

मयि सर्वाणि कर्माणि सन्न्यस्याध्यात्मचेतसा।
निराशीर्निर्ममो भूत्वा युध्यस्व विगतज्वरः॥ ३०॥

Therefore, dedicating all actions to Me with your mind fixed on Me, the Self of all, freed from desire and the feeling of meum and cured of mental agitation, fight. (30)

ये मे मतमिदं नित्यमनुतिष्ठन्ति मानवाः।
श्रद्धावन्तोऽनसूयन्तो मुच्यन्ते तेऽपि कर्मभिः॥ ३१॥

Even those men who, with an uncavilling and devout mind, always follow this teaching of Mine, are released from the bondage of all actions. (31)

ये त्वेतदभ्यसूयन्तो नानुतिष्ठन्ति मे मतम्।
सर्वज्ञानविमूढांस्तान्विद्धि नष्टानचेतसः॥ ३२॥

But they, however, who, finding fault with this teaching of Mine, do not follow it, take those fools to be deluded in the matter of all knowledge as lost. (32)

सदृशं चेष्टते स्वस्याः प्रकृतेर्ज्ञानवानपि।
प्रकृतिं यान्ति भूतानि निग्रहः किं करिष्यति॥ ३३॥

All living creatures follow their tendencies; even the wise man acts according to the tendencies of his own nature. Of what use is restraint by force. (33)

इन्द्रियस्येन्द्रियस्यार्थे रागद्वेषौ व्यवस्थितौ।
तयोर्न वशमागच्छेत्तौ ह्यस्य परिपन्थिनौ॥ ३४॥

Attraction and repulsion are rooted in all sense-objects. Man should never allow himself to be swayed by them, because they are the two principal enemies standing in the way of his redemption. (34)

श्रेयान्स्वधर्मो विगुणः परधर्मात्स्वनुष्ठितात्।
स्वधर्मे निधनं श्रेयः परधर्मो भयावहः॥ ३५॥

One's own duty, though devoid of merit, is preferable to the duty of another well performed. Even death in the performance of one's own duty brings blessedness; another's duty is fraught with fear. (35)

अर्जुन उवाच

अथ केन प्रयुक्तोऽयं पापं चरति पूरुषः।
अनिच्छन्नपि वार्ष्णेय बलादिव नियोजितः॥ ३६॥

Arjuna said : Now impelled by what, Kṛṣṇa, does this man commit sin even involuntarily, as though driven by force? (36)

श्रीभगवानुवाच

काम एष क्रोध एष रजोगुणसमुद्भवः।
महाशनो महापाप्मा विद्ध्येनमिह वैरिणम्॥ ३७॥

Śrī Bhagavān said : It is desire begotten of the element of Rajas, which appears as wrath; nay, it is insatiable and grossly wicked. Know this to be the enemy in this case. (37)

धूमेनाव्रियते वह्निर्यथादर्शो मलेन च।
यथोल्बेनावृतो गर्भस्तथा तेनेदमावृतम्॥ ३८॥

As fire is covered by smoke, mirror by dust, and embryo by the amnion, so is knowledge covered by desire. (38)

आवृतं ज्ञानमेतेन ज्ञानिनो नित्यवैरिणा।
कामरूपेण कौन्तेय दुष्पूरेणानलेन च॥ ३९॥

And, Arjuna, Knowledge stands covered by this eternal enemy of the wise, known as desire, which is insatiable like fire. (39)

इन्द्रियाणि मनो बुद्धिरस्याधिष्ठानमुच्यते।
एतैर्विमोहयत्येष ज्ञानमावृत्य देहिनम्॥ ४०॥

The senses, the mind and the intellect are declared to be its seat; covering the knowledge through these, it (desire) deludes the embodied soul. (40)

तस्मात्त्वमिन्द्रियाण्यादौ नियम्य भरतर्षभ।
पाप्मानं प्रजहि ह्येनं ज्ञानविज्ञाननाशनम्॥ ४१॥

Therefore, Arjuna, you must first control your senses, and then kill this evil thing which obstructs Jñāna (Knowledge of the Absolute or Nirguṇa Brahma) and Vijñāna (Knowledge of Sākāra Brahma or manifest Divinity). (41)

इन्द्रियाणि पराण्याहुरिन्द्रियेभ्यः परं मनः।
मनसस्तु परा बुद्धिर्यो बुद्धेः परतस्तु सः॥ ४२॥

The senses are said to be greater than the body; but greater than the senses is the mind. Greater than the mind is the intellect; and what is greater than the intellect is He, the Self. (42)

एवं बुद्धेः परं बुद्ध्वा संस्तभ्यात्मानमात्मना।
जहि शत्रुं महाबाहो कामरूपं दुरासदम्॥ ४३॥

Thus, Arjuna, knowing the Self which is higher than the intellect and subduing the mind by reason, kill this enemy in the form of desire that is hard to overcome. (43)

ॐ तत्सदिति श्रीमद्भगवद्गीतासूपनिषत्सु ब्रह्मविद्यायां
योगशास्त्रे श्रीकृष्णार्जुनसंवादे कर्मयोगो नाम
तृतीयोऽध्यायः॥ ३॥

Thus, in the Upaniṣad sung by the Lord, the Science of Brahma, the scripture of Yoga, the dialogue between Śrī Kṛṣṇa and Arjuna, ends the third chapter entitled "Karmayoga, or the Yoga of Action."

Chapter IV

श्रीभगवानुवाच

इमं विवस्वते योगं प्रोक्तवानहमव्ययम्।
विवस्वान्मनवे प्राह मनुरिक्ष्वाकवेऽब्रवीत्॥ १॥

Śrī Bhagavān said: I revealed this immortal Yoga to Vivasvān (Sun-god); Vivasvān conveyed it to Manu (his son); and Manu imparted it to (his son) Ikṣvāku. (1)

एवं परम्पराप्राप्तमिमं राजर्षयो विदुः।
स कालेनेह महता योगो नष्टः परन्तप॥ २॥

Thus transmitted in succession from father to son, Arjuna, this Yoga remained known to the Rājarṣis (royal sages). Through long lapse of time, this Yoga got lost to the world. (2)

स एवायं मया तेऽद्य योगः प्रोक्तः पुरातनः।
भक्तोऽसि मे सखा चेति रहस्यं ह्येतदुत्तमम्॥ ३॥

The same ancient Yoga, which is the supreme secret, has this day been imparted to you by Me, because you are My devotee and friend. (3)

अर्जुन उवाच

अपरं भवतो जन्म परं जन्म विवस्वतः।
कथमेतद्विजानीयां त्वमादौ प्रोक्तवानिति॥ ४॥

Arjuna said: You are of recent origin, while

the birth of Vivasvān dates back to remote antiquity. How, then, am I to believe that You imparted this Yoga at the beginning of the creation? (4)

श्रीभगवानुवाच

बहूनि मे व्यतीतानि जन्मानि तव चार्जुन।
तान्यहं वेद सर्वाणि न त्वं वेत्थ परन्तप॥ ५॥

Śrī Bhagavān said: Arjuna, you and I have passed through many births; I remember them all; you do not remember, O chastiser of foes. (5)

अजोऽपि सन्नव्ययात्मा भूतानामीश्वरोऽपि सन्।
प्रकृतिं स्वामधिष्ठाय सम्भवाम्यात्ममायया॥ ६॥

Though birthless and immortal and the Lord of all beings, I manifest Myself through My own Yogamāyā (divine potency), keeping My nature (Prakṛti) under control. (6)

यदा यदा हि धर्मस्य ग्लानिर्भवति भारत।
अभ्युत्थानमधर्मस्य तदात्मानं सृजाम्यहम्॥ ७॥

Arjuna, whenever righteousness is on the decline, unrighteousness is in the ascendant, then I body Myself forth. (7)

परित्राणाय साधूनां विनाशाय च दुष्कृताम्।
धर्मसंस्थापनार्थाय सम्भवामि युगे युगे॥ ८॥

For the protection of the virtuous, for the extirpation of evil-doers, and for establishing Dharma (righteousness) on a firm footing, I manifest Myself from age to age. (8)

जन्म कर्म च मे दिव्यमेवं यो वेत्ति तत्त्वतः।
त्यक्त्वा देहं पुनर्जन्म नैति मामेति सोऽर्जुन॥ ९ ॥

Arjuna, My birth and activities are divine. He who knows this in reality is not reborn on leaving his body, but comes to Me. (9)

वीतरागभयक्रोधा मन्मया मामुपाश्रिताः।
बहवो ज्ञानतपसा पूता मद्भावमागताः॥ १० ॥

Completely rid of attachment, fear and anger, wholly absorbed in Me, depending on Me, and purified by the penance of wisdom, many have become one with Me even in the past. (10)

ये यथा मां प्रपद्यन्ते तांस्तथैव भजाम्यहम्।
मम वर्त्मानुवर्तन्ते मनुष्याः पार्थ सर्वशः॥ ११ ॥

Arjuna, howsoever men seek Me, even so do I respond to them; for all men follow My path in everyway. (11)

काङ्क्षन्तः कर्मणां सिद्धिं यजन्त इह देवताः।
क्षिप्रं हि मानुषे लोके सिद्धिर्भवति कर्मजा॥ १२ ॥

In this world of human beings, men seeking the fruition of their activities, worship the gods; for success born of actions follows quickly. (12)

चातुर्वर्ण्यं मया सृष्टं गुणकर्मविभागशः।
तस्य कर्तारमपि मां विद्ध्यकर्तारमव्ययम्॥ १३ ॥

The four orders of society (viz., the Brāhmaṇa, the Kṣatriya, the Vaiśya and the Śūdra) were created by Me, classifying them according to the Guṇas predominant in each and apportioning corresponding duties to them; though the originator of this creation, know Me, the Immortal Lord, to be a non-doer. (13)

न मां कर्माणि लिम्पन्ति न मे कर्मफले स्पृहा।
इति मां योऽभिजानाति कर्मभिर्न स बध्यते॥ १४॥

Since I have no craving for the fruit of actions, actions do not taint Me. Even he who thus knows Me in reality is not bound by actions. (14)

एवं ज्ञात्वा कृतं कर्म पूर्वैरपि मुमुक्षुभिः।
कुरु कर्मैव तस्मात्त्वं पूर्वैः पूर्वतरं कृतम्॥ १५॥

Having known thus, action was performed even by the ancient seekers for liberation; therefore, do you also perform actions as have been performed by the ancients from antiquity. (15)

किं कर्म किमकर्मेति कवयोऽप्यत्र मोहिताः।
तत्ते कर्म प्रवक्ष्यामि यज्ज्ञात्वा मोक्ष्यसेऽशुभात्॥ १६॥

What is action and what is inaction? Even men of intelligence are puzzled over this question. Therefore, I shall expound to you the truth about action, knowing which you will be freed from its evil effects i.e., the shackles of karma. (16)

कर्मणो ह्यपि बोद्धव्यं बोद्धव्यं च विकर्मणः।
अकर्मणश्च बोद्धव्यं गहना कर्मणो गतिः॥ १७॥

The truth about action must be known and the truth of inaction also must be known; even so, the truth about prohibited action (Vikarma) must be known. For, mysterious are the ways of action. (17)

कर्मण्यकर्म यः पश्येदकर्मणि च कर्म यः।
स बुद्धिमान्मनुष्येषु स युक्तः कृत्स्नकर्मकृत्॥ १८॥

He who sees inaction in action, and action in inaction, is wise among men; he is a Yogī, who has performed all actions. (18)

यस्य सर्वे समारम्भाः कामसङ्कल्पवर्जिताः।
ज्ञानाग्निदग्धकर्माणं तमाहुः पण्डितं बुधाः॥ १९॥

Even the wise call him a sage, whose undertakings are all free from desire and Saṅkalpa (thoughts of the world) and whose actions are burnt up by the fire of wisdom. (19)

त्यक्त्वा कर्मफलासङ्गं नित्यतृप्तो निराश्रयः।
कर्मण्यभिप्रवृत्तोऽपि नैव किञ्चित्करोति सः॥ २०॥

He, who, having totally given up attachment to actions and their fruit, no longer depends on anything in the world, and is ever content, does nothing at all, though fully engaged in action. (20)

निराशीर्यतचित्तात्मा त्यक्तसर्वपरिग्रहः।
शारीरं केवलं कर्म कुर्वन्नाप्नोति किल्बिषम्॥ २१॥

Having subdued his mind and body, and having given up all objects of enjoyment, free from craving, he who performs sheer bodily action, does not incur sin. (21)

यदृच्छालाभसन्तुष्टो द्वन्द्वातीतो विमत्सरः।
समः सिद्धावसिद्धौ च कृत्वापि न निबध्यते॥ २२॥

The Karmayogī, who is contented with

whatever is got unsought, is free from jealousy and has transcended all pairs of opposites like joy and grief, and is balanced in success and failure, is not bound by his action. (22)

गतसङ्गस्य मुक्तस्य ज्ञानावस्थितचेतसः।
यज्ञायाचरतः कर्म समग्रं प्रविलीयते॥ २३॥

All his actions get dissolved entirely, who is free from attachment and has no identification with the body and free from the feeling of mine, whose mind is established in the knowledge of Self and who works merely for the sake of sacrifice. (23)

ब्रह्मार्पणं ब्रह्म हविर्ब्रह्माग्नौ ब्रह्मणा हुतम्।
ब्रह्मैव तेन गन्तव्यं ब्रह्मकर्मसमाधिना॥ २४॥

In the practice of seeing Brahma everywhere as a form of sacrifice, Brahma is the ladle (with which oblation is poured into the fire, etc.); Brahma, again, is the oblation; Brahma is the fire, Brahma itself is the sacrificer and so Brahma itself constitutes the act of pouring the oblation into the fire. And, finally, Brahma is the goal to be reached by him who is absorbed in Brahma as the act of such sacrifice. (24)

दैवमेवापरे यज्ञं योगिनः पर्युपासते।
ब्रह्माग्नावपरे यज्ञं यज्ञेनैवोपजुह्वति॥ २५॥

Other Yogīs duly offer sacrifice only in the form of worship to gods, while others perform sacrifice by offering the self by the Self itself in the fire of Brahma. (25)

श्रोत्रादीनीन्द्रियाण्यन्ये संयमाग्निषु जुह्वति।
शब्दादीन्विषयानन्य इन्द्रियाग्निषु जुह्वति॥ २६॥

Others offer as sacrifice their senses of hearing etc., into the fires of self-discipline. Other Yogīs, again, offer sound and other objects of perception into the fires of the senses. (26)

सर्वाणीन्द्रियकर्माणि प्राणकर्माणि चापरे।
आत्मसंयमयोगाग्नौ जुह्वति ज्ञानदीपिते॥ २७॥

Others sacrifice all the functions of their senses and the functions of the vital airs (Prāṇa) into the fire of Yoga in the shape of self-control, kindled by wisdom. (27)

द्रव्ययज्ञास्तपोयज्ञा योगयज्ञास्तथापरे।
स्वाध्यायज्ञानयज्ञाश्च यतयः संशितव्रताः॥ २८॥

Some perform sacrifice with material possessions; some offer sacrifice in the shape of austerities; others sacrifice through the practice of Yoga; while some striving souls, observing austere vows, perform sacrifice in the shape of wisdom through the study of sacred texts. (28)

अपाने जुह्वति प्राणं प्राणेऽपानं तथापरे।
प्राणापानगती रुद्ध्वा प्राणायामपरायणाः॥ २९॥
अपरे नियताहाराः प्राणान्प्राणेषु जुह्वति।
सर्वेऽप्येते यज्ञविदो यज्ञक्षपितकल्मषाः॥ ३०॥

Other Yogīs offer the act of exhalation into

that of inhalation; even so, others the act of inhalation into that of exhalation. There are still others given to the practice of Prāṇāyāma (breath-control), who, having regulated their diet and controlled the processes of exhalation and inhalation both, pour their vital airs into the vital airs themselves. All these have their sins consumed away by sacrifice and understand the meaning of sacrificial worship. (29-30)

यज्ञशिष्टामृतभुजो यान्ति ब्रह्म सनातनम्।
नायं लोकोऽस्त्ययज्ञस्य कुतोऽन्यः कुरुसत्तम॥ ३१॥

Arjuna, Yogīs who enjoy the nectar that has been left over after the performance of a sacrifice attain the eternal Brahma. To the man who does not offer sacrifice, even this world is not happy; how, then, can the other world be happy? (31)

एवं बहुविधा यज्ञा वितता ब्रह्मणो मुखे।
कर्मजान्विद्धि तान्सर्वानेवं ज्ञात्वा विमोक्ष्यसे॥ ३२॥

Many such forms of sacrifice have been set forth in detail in the Vedas; know them all as involving the action of mind, senses and body. Thus, knowing the truth about them you shall be freed from the bondage of action (through their performance). (32)

श्रेयान्द्रव्यमयाद्यज्ञाज्ज्ञानयज्ञः परन्तप।
सर्वं कर्माखिलं पार्थ ज्ञाने परिसमाप्यते॥ ३३॥

Arjuna, sacrifice through Knowledge, is superior to sacrifice performed with material things. For all actions without exception culminate in Knowledge, O son of Kuntī. (33)

तद्विद्धि प्रणिपातेन परिप्रश्नेन सेवया।
उपदेक्ष्यन्ति ते ज्ञानं ज्ञानिनस्तत्त्वदर्शिनः॥ ३४॥

Understand the true nature of that Knowledge by approaching seers of Truth. If you prostrate at their feet, render them service, and question them with an open and guileless heart, those wise seers of Truth will instruct you in that Knowledge.(34)

यज्ज्ञात्वा न पुनर्मोहमेवं यास्यसि पाण्डव।
येन भूतान्यशेषेण द्रक्ष्यस्यात्मन्यथो मयि॥ ३५॥

Arjuna, when you have achieved enlightenment, ignorance will delude you no more. In the light of that knowledge, you will see the entire creation first within your own Self, and then in Me (the Oversoul). (35)

अपि चेदसि पापेभ्यः सर्वेभ्यः पापकृत्तमः।
सर्वं ज्ञानप्लवेनैव वृजिनं सन्तरिष्यसि॥ ३६॥

Even if you were the most sinful of all sinners, this Knowledge alone would carry you, like a raft, across all your sins. (36)

यथैधांसि समिद्धोऽग्निर्भस्मसात्कुरुतेऽर्जुन।
ज्ञानाग्निः सर्वकर्माणि भस्मसात्कुरुते तथा॥ ३७॥

For, as the blazing fire reduces the fuel to ashes, Arjuna, even so the fire of Knowledge turns all actions to ashes. (37)

न हि ज्ञानेन सदृशं पवित्रमिह विद्यते।
तत्स्वयं योगसंसिद्धः कालेनात्मनि विन्दति॥ ३८॥

In this world there is no purifier as great as Knowledge; he who has attained purity of heart through prolonged practice of Karmayoga, automatically sees the light of Truth in the self in course of time. (38)

श्रद्धावाँल्लभते ज्ञानं तत्परः संयतेन्द्रियः।
ज्ञानं लब्ध्वा परां शान्तिमचिरेणाधिगच्छति॥ ३९॥

He who has mastered his senses, is exclusively devoted to his practice and is full of faith, attains Knowledge; having had the revelation of Truth, he immediately attains supreme peace in the form of God-realization. (39)

अज्ञश्चाश्रद्दधानश्च संशयात्मा विनश्यति।
नायं लोकोऽस्ति न परो न सुखं संशयात्मनः॥ ४०॥

He who lacks discrimination, is devoid of faith, and is at the same time possessed by doubt, is lost to the spiritual path. For the doubting soul there is neither this world nor the world beyond, nor even happiness. (40)

योगसन्न्यस्तकर्माणं ज्ञानसञ्छिन्नसंशयम्।
आत्मवन्तं न कर्माणि निबध्नन्ति धनञ्जय॥ ४१॥

Arjuna, actions do not bind him who has dedicated all his actions to God according to the spirit of Karmayoga, whose doubts have been dispelled by wisdom and who is self-possessed. (41)

तस्मादज्ञानसम्भूतं हृत्स्थं ज्ञानासिनात्मनः।
छित्त्वैनं संशयं योगमातिष्ठोत्तिष्ठ भारत॥ ४२॥

Therefore, Arjuna slashing to pieces, with the sword of knowledge, this doubt in your heart, born of ignorance, establish yourself in Karmayoga in the shape of even-mindedness, and stand up for the fight. (42)

ॐ तत्सदिति श्रीमद्भगवद्गीतासूपनिषत्सु ब्रह्मविद्यायां योगशास्त्रे श्रीकृष्णार्जुनसंवादे ज्ञानकर्मसन्न्यासयोगो नाम चतुर्थोऽध्यायः॥ ४॥

Thus, in the Upaniṣad sung by the Lord, the Science of Brahma, the scripture of Yoga, the dialogue between Śrī Kṛṣṇa and Arjuna, ends the fourth chapter entitled "The Yoga of Knowledge as well as the disciplines of Action and Knowledge."

Chapter V

अर्जुन उवाच

सन्न्यासं कर्मणां कृष्ण पुनर्योगं च शंससि।
यच्छ्रेय एतयोरेकं तन्मे ब्रूहि सुनिश्चितम्॥ १॥

Arjuna said : Kṛṣṇa, you extol Sāṅkhyayoga (the Yoga of Knowledge) and then the Yoga of Action. Pray, tell me which of the two is decidedly conducive to my good. (1)

श्रीभगवानुवाच

सन्न्यासः कर्मयोगश्च निःश्रेयसकरावुभौ।
तयोस्तु कर्मसन्न्यासात्कर्मयोगो विशिष्यते॥ २॥

Śrī Bhagavān said : The Yoga of Knowledge and the Yoga of Action both lead to supreme Bliss. Of the two, however, the Yoga of Action, being easier of practice, is superior to the Yoga of Knowledge. (2)

ज्ञेयः स नित्यसन्न्यासी यो न द्वेष्टि न काङ्क्षति।
निर्द्वन्द्वो हि महाबाहो सुखं बन्धात्प्रमुच्यते॥ ३॥

The Karmayogī who neither hates nor desires should ever be considered as an ever renunciant. For, Arjuna, he who is free from the pairs of opposites is easily liberated from bondage. (3)

साङ्ख्ययोगौ पृथग्बालाः प्रवदन्ति न पण्डिताः।
एकमप्यास्थितः सम्यगुभयोर्विन्दते फलम्॥ ४॥

It is the ignorant, not the wise, who say that Sāṅkhyayoga and Karmayoga lead to divergent results. For, one who is firmly established in either, gets the fruit of both which is the same, viz., God-realization. (4)

यत्साङ्ख्यैः प्राप्यते स्थानं तद्योगैरपि गम्यते।
एकं साङ्ख्यं च योगं च यः पश्यति स पश्यति॥ ५॥

The (supreme) state which is reached by the Sāṅkhyayogī is attained also by the Karmayogī. Therefore, he alone who sees Sāṅkhyayoga and Karmayoga as identical so far as their result goes, sees truly. (5)

सन्न्यासस्तु महाबाहो दुःखमाप्तुमयोगतः।
योगयुक्तो मुनिर्ब्रह्म नचिरेणाधिगच्छति॥ ६॥

Without Karmayoga, however, Sāṅkhyayoga i.e., renunciation of doership in relation to all activities of the mind, senses and body is difficult to accomplish; whereas the Karmayogī, who keeps his mind fixed on God, reaches Brahma in no time, Arjuna. (6)

योगयुक्तो विशुद्धात्मा विजितात्मा जितेन्द्रियः।
सर्वभूतात्मभूतात्मा कुर्वन्नपि न लिप्यते॥ ७॥

The Karmayogī, who has fully conquered his mind and mastered his senses, whose heart is pure, and who has identified himself with the Self of all beings (viz., God), remains untainted, even though performing action. (7)

नैव किञ्चित्करोमीति युक्तो मन्येत तत्त्ववित्।
पश्यञ्शृण्वन्स्पृशञ्जिघ्रन्नश्नन्गच्छन्स्वपञ्श्वसन्॥ ८ ॥
प्रलपन्विसृजन्गृह्णन्नुन्मिषन्निमिषन्नपि ।
इन्द्रियाणीन्द्रियार्थेषु वर्तन्त इति धारयन्॥ ९ ॥

However, the Sāṅkhyayogī, who knows the reality of things, must believe that he does nothing, even though seeing, hearing, touching, smelling, eating or drinking, walking, sleeping, breathing, speaking, answering the calls of nature, grasping, and opening or closing the eyes, holding that it is the senses alone that are moving among their objects. (8-9)

ब्रह्मण्याधाय कर्माणि सङ्गं त्यक्त्वा करोति यः।
लिप्यते न स पापेन पद्मपत्रमिवाम्भसा॥ १० ॥

He who acts offering all actions to God, and shaking off attachment, remains untouched by sin, as the lotus leaf by water. (10)

कायेन मनसा बुद्ध्या केवलैरिन्द्रियैरपि।
योगिनः कर्म कुर्वन्ति सङ्गं त्यक्त्वात्मशुद्धये॥ ११ ॥

The Karmayogīs perform action only with their senses, mind, intellect and body as well, without the feeling of mine in respect of them and shaking off attachment, simply for the sake of self-purification. (11)

युक्तः कर्मफलं त्यक्त्वा शान्तिमाप्नोति नैष्ठिकीम्।
अयुक्तः कामकारेण फले सक्तो निबध्यते॥ १२ ॥

Offering the fruit of actions to God, the Karmayogī attains everlasting peace in the form of God-realization; whereas, he who works with a selfish motive, being attached to the fruit of actions through desire, gets tied down. (12)

सर्वकर्माणि मनसा सन्न्यस्यास्ते सुखं वशी।
नवद्वारे पुरे देही नैव कुर्वन्न कारयन्॥ १३॥

The self-controlled Sāṅkhyayogī, doing nothing himself and getting nothing done by others, rests happily in God—the embodiment of Truth, Knowledge and Bliss, mentally relegating all actions to the mansion of nine gates (the body with nine openings). (13)

न कर्तृत्वं न कर्माणि लोकस्य सृजति प्रभुः।
न कर्मफलसंयोगं स्वभावस्तु प्रवर्तते॥ १४॥

God determines neither the doership nor the doings of men, nor even their contact with the fruit of actions; but it is Nature alone that does all this. (14)

नादत्ते कस्यचित्पापं न चैव सुकृतं विभुः।
अज्ञानेनावृतं ज्ञानं तेन मुह्यन्ति जन्तवः॥ १५॥

The omnipresent God does not partake the virtue or sin of anyone. Knowledge is enveloped by ignorance; hence it is that beings are constantly falling a prey to delusion. (15)

ज्ञानेन तु तदज्ञानं येषां नाशितमात्मनः।
तेषामादित्यवज्ज्ञानं प्रकाशयति तत्परम्॥ १६॥

In the case, however, of those whose said ignorance has been destroyed by true knowledge of God, that wisdom shining like the sun reveals the Supreme. (16)

तद्बुद्धयस्तदात्मानस्तन्निष्ठास्तत्परायणाः ।
गच्छन्त्यपुनरावृत्तिं ज्ञाननिर्धूतकल्मषाः ॥ १७ ॥

Those whose mind and intellect are wholly merged in Him, who remain constantly established in identity with Him, and have finally become one with Him, their sins being wiped out by wisdom, reach the supreme goal whence there is no return. (17)

विद्याविनयसम्पन्ने ब्राह्मणे गवि हस्तिनि ।
शुनि चैव श्वपाके च पण्डिताः समदर्शिनः ॥ १८ ॥

The wise look with equanimity on all whether it be a Brāhmaṇa endowed with learning and humility, a cow, an elephant, a dog and a pariah, too. (18)

इहैव तैर्जितः सर्गो येषां साम्ये स्थितं मनः ।
निर्दोषं हि समं ब्रह्म तस्माद्ब्रह्मणि ते स्थिताः ॥ १९ ॥

Even here is the mortal plane conquered by those whose mind is established in equanimity; since the Absolute is untouched by evil and is the same to all, hence they are established in Paramātmā. (19)

न प्रहृष्येत्प्रियं प्राप्य नोद्विजेत्प्राप्य चाप्रियम् ।
स्थिरबुद्धिरसम्मूढो ब्रह्मविद् ब्रह्मणि स्थितः ॥ २० ॥

He who, with firm intellect and free from doubt, rejoices not on obtaining what is pleasant and does not feel perturbed on meeting with the unpleasant, that knower of Brahma lives eternally in identity with Brahma. (20)

बाह्यस्पर्शेष्वसक्तात्मा विन्दत्यात्मनि यत्सुखम्।
स ब्रह्मयोगयुक्तात्मा सुखमक्षयमश्नुते ॥ २१ ॥

He whose mind remains unattached to sense-objects, derives through meditation, the Sāttvika joy which dwells in the mind; then that Yogī, having completely identified himself through meditation with Brahma, enjoys eternal Bliss. (21)

ये हि संस्पर्शजा भोगा दुःखयोनय एव ते।
आद्यन्तवन्तः कौन्तेय न तेषु रमते बुधः ॥ २२ ॥

The pleasures which are born of sense-contacts, are verily a source of suffering only (though appearing as enjoyable to worldly-minded people). They have a beginning and an end (they come and go); Arjuna, it is for this reason that a wise man does not indulge in them. (22)

शक्नोतीहैव यः सोढुं प्राक्शरीरविमोक्षणात्।
कामक्रोधोद्भवं वेगं स युक्तः स सुखी नरः ॥ २३ ॥

He alone, who is able to withstand, in this very life before casting off this body, the urges of lust and anger, is a Yogī, and he alone is a happy man. (23)

योऽन्तःसुखोऽन्तरारामस्तथान्तर्ज्योतिरेव यः।
स योगी ब्रह्मनिर्वाणं ब्रह्मभूतोऽधिगच्छति ॥ २४ ॥

He who is happy within himself, enjoys within himself the delight of the soul, and, even so, is illumined by the inner light (light of the soul), such a Yogī (Sāṅkhyayogī) identified with Brahma attains Brahma, who is all peace. (24)

लभन्ते ब्रह्मनिर्वाणमृषयः क्षीणकल्मषाः ।
छिन्नद्वैधा यतात्मानः सर्वभूतहिते रताः ॥ २५ ॥

The seers whose sins have been purged, whose doubts have been dispelled by knowledge, whose disciplined mind is firmly established in God and who are devoted to the welfare of all beings, attain Brahma, who is all peace. (25)

कामक्रोधवियुक्तानां यतीनां यतचेतसाम् ।
अभितो ब्रह्मनिर्वाणं वर्तते विदितात्मनाम् ॥ २६ ॥

To those wise men who are free from lust and anger, who have subdued their mind and have realized God, Brahma, the abode of eternal peace, is present all-round. (26)

स्पर्शान्कृत्वा बहिर्बाह्यांश्चक्षुश्चैवान्तरे भ्रुवोः ।
प्राणापानौ समौ कृत्वा नासाभ्यन्तरचारिणौ ॥ २७ ॥
यतेन्द्रियमनोबुद्धिर्मुनिर्मोक्षपरायणः ।
विगतेच्छाभयक्रोधो यः सदा मुक्त एव सः ॥ २८ ॥

Shutting out all thoughts of external enjoyments, with the gaze fixed on the space between the eye-brows, having regulated the Prāṇa (outgoing) and the Apāna (incoming) breaths flowing within the nostrils, he who has brought his senses, mind and intellect under control—such a contemplative soul intent on liberation and free from desire, fear and anger, is ever liberated. (27-28)

भोक्तारं यज्ञतपसां सर्वलोकमहेश्वरम्।
सुहृदं सर्वभूतानां ज्ञात्वा मां शान्तिमृच्छति॥ २९॥

Having known Me in reality as the enjoyer of all sacrifices and austerities, the supreme Lord of all the worlds, and the selfless friend of all beings, My devotee attains peace. (29)

ॐ तत्सदिति श्रीमद्भगवद्गीतासूपनिषत्सु ब्रह्मविद्यायां
योगशास्त्रे श्रीकृष्णार्जुनसंवादे कर्मसन्न्यासयोगो
नाम पञ्चमोऽध्याय:॥ ५॥

Thus, in the Upaniṣad sung by the Lord, the Science of Brahma, the scripture of Yoga, the dialogue between Śrī Kṛṣṇa and Arjuna, ends the fifth chapter entitled "The Yoga of Action and Knowledge."

Chapter VI

श्रीभगवानुवाच

अनाश्रितः कर्मफलं कार्यं कर्म करोति यः।
स सन्न्यासी च योगी च न निरग्निर्न चाक्रियः॥ १॥

Śrī Bhagavān said : He who does his duty without expecting the fruit of actions is a Sannyāsī (Sāṅkhyayogī) and a Yogī (Karmayogī) both. He is no Sannyāsī (renouncer) who has merely renounced the sacred fire; even so, he is no Yogī who has merely given up all activity. (1)

यं सन्न्यासमिति प्राहुर्योगं तं विद्धि पाण्डव।
न ह्यसन्न्यस्तसङ्कल्पो योगी भवति कश्चन॥ २॥

Arjuna, you must know that what they call Sannyāsa is no other than Yoga; for none becomes a Yogī, who has not abandoned his 'Saṅkalpas' (thoughts of the world). (2)

आरुरुक्षोर्मुनेर्योगं कर्म कारणमुच्यते।
योगारूढस्य तस्यैव शमः कारणमुच्यते॥ ३॥

To the contemplative soul who desires to attain Karmayoga, selfless action is said to be the means; for the same man when he is established in Yoga, absence of all 'Saṅkalpas' (thoughts of the world) is said to be the way to blessedness. (3)

यदा हि नेन्द्रियार्थेषु न कर्मस्वनुषज्जते।
सर्वसङ्कल्पसन्न्यासी योगारूढस्तदोच्यते॥ ४॥

When a man ceases to have any attachment for the objects of senses and for actions, and has renounced all 'Saṅkalpas' (thoughts of the world), he is said to have attained Yoga. (4)

उद्धरेदात्मनात्मानं नात्मानमवसादयेत्।
आत्मैव ह्यात्मनो बन्धुरात्मैव रिपुरात्मनः॥ ५॥

One should lift oneself by one's own efforts and should not degrade oneself; for one's own self is one's friend, and one's own self is one's enemy. (5)

बन्धुरात्मात्मनस्तस्य येनात्मैवात्मना जितः।
अनात्मनस्तु शत्रुत्वे वर्तेतात्मैव शत्रुवत्॥ ६॥

One's own Self is the friend of the soul by whom the lower self (consisting of the mind, senses and body) has been conquered; even so, the very Self of him, who has not conquered his lower self, behaves antagonistically like an enemy. (6)

जितात्मनः प्रशान्तस्य परमात्मा समाहितः।
शीतोष्णसुखदुःखेषु तथा मानापमानयोः॥ ७॥

The Supreme Spirit is rooted in the knowledge of the self-controlled man whose mind is perfectly serene in the midst of pairs of opposites, such as cold and heat, joy and sorrow, and honour and ignominy. (7)

ज्ञानविज्ञानतृप्तात्मा कूटस्थो विजितेन्द्रियः।
युक्त इत्युच्यते योगी समलोष्टाश्मकाञ्चनः॥ ८॥

The Yogī whose mind is sated with Jñāna (Knowledge of Nirguṇa Brahma) and Vijñāna (Knowledge of manifest Divinity), who is unmoved under any circumstances, whose senses are completely under control, and to whom earth, stone and gold are all alike, is spoken of as a God-realized soul. (8)

सुहृन्मित्रार्युदासीनमध्यस्थद्वेष्यबन्धुषु।
साधुष्वपि च पापेषु समबुद्धिर्विशिष्यते॥ ९॥

He who looks upon well-wishers and neutrals as well as mediators, friends and foes, relatives and inimicals, the virtuous and the sinful with equanimity, stands supreme. (9)

योगी युञ्जीत सततमात्मानं रहसि स्थितः।
एकाकी यतचित्तात्मा निराशीरपरिग्रहः॥ १०॥

Living in seclusion all by himself, the Yogī who has controlled his mind and body, and is free from desires and void of possessions, should constantly engage his mind in meditation. (10)

शुचौ देशे प्रतिष्ठाप्य स्थिरमासनमात्मनः।
नात्युच्छ्रितं नातिनीचं चैलाजिनकुशोत्तरम्॥ ११॥

Having firmly set his seat in a spot which is free from dirt and other impurities with the sacred Kuśa grass, a deerskin and a cloth spread thereon, one upon the other, (Kuśa below, deerskin in the middle and cloth uppermost), neither very high nor very low; (11)

तत्रैकाग्रं मनः कृत्वा यतचित्तेन्द्रियक्रियः।
उपविश्यासने युञ्ज्याद्योगमात्मविशुद्धये॥ १२॥

And, occupying that seat, concentrating the mind and controlling the functions of the mind and senses, he should practise Yoga for self-purification. (12)

समं कायशिरोग्रीवं धारयन्नचलं स्थिरः।
सम्प्रेक्ष्य नासिकाग्रं स्वं दिशश्चानवलोकयन्॥ १३॥

Holding the trunk, head and neck straight and steady, remaining firm and fixing the gaze on the tip of his nose, without looking in other directions. (13)

प्रशान्तात्मा विगतभीर्ब्रह्मचारिव्रते स्थितः।
मनः संयम्य मच्चित्तो युक्त आसीत मत्परः॥ १४॥

Firm in the vow of complete chastity and fearless, keeping himself perfectly calm and with the mind held in restraint and fixed on Me, the vigilant Yogī should sit absorbed in Me. (14)

युञ्जन्नेवं सदात्मानं योगी नियतमानसः।
शान्तिं निर्वाणपरमां मत्संस्थामधिगच्छति॥ १५॥

Thus, constantly applying his mind to Me, the Yogī of disciplined mind, attains everlasting peace, consisting of Supreme Bliss, which abides in Me. (15)

नात्यश्नतस्तु योगोऽस्ति न चैकान्तमनश्नतः।
न चाति स्वप्नशीलस्य जाग्रतो नैव चार्जुन॥ १६॥

Arjuna, this Yoga is neither for him who overeats, nor for him who observes complete fast; it is neither for him who is given to too much sleep, nor even for him who is ceaselessly awake. (16)

युक्ताहारविहारस्य युक्तचेष्टस्य कर्मसु।
युक्तस्वप्नावबोधस्य योगो भवति दुःखहा॥ १७॥

Yoga, which rids one of woe, is accomplished only by him who is regulated in diet and recreation, regulated in performing actions, and regulated in sleep and wakefulness. (17)

यदा विनियतं चित्तमात्मन्येवावतिष्ठते।
निःस्पृहः सर्वकामेभ्यो युक्त इत्युच्यते तदा॥ १८॥

When the mind which is thoroughly disciplined, gets riveted on God alone, then the person who is free from yearning for all enjoyments is said to be established in Yoga. (18)

यथा दीपो निवातस्थो नेङ्गते सोपमा स्मृता।
योगिनो यतचित्तस्य युञ्जतो योगमात्मनः॥ १९॥

As a flame does not flicker in a windless place, such is stated to be the picture of the disciplined mind of the Yogī practising meditation on God. (19)

यत्रोपरमते चित्तं निरुद्धं योगसेवया।
यत्र चैवात्मनात्मानं पश्यन्नात्मनि तुष्यति॥ २०॥

The state in which the Citta (mind-stuff) subdued through the practice of Yoga, becomes completely tranquil, and in which realizing God through subtle reasoning purified by meditation on God, the soul rejoices only in God; (20)

सुखमात्यन्तिकं यत्तद्बुद्धिग्राह्यमतीन्द्रियम्।
वेत्ति यत्र न चैवायं स्थितश्चलति तत्त्वतः॥ २१॥

Nay, in which the soul experiences the eternal and super-sensuous joy which can be intuited only through the subtle and purified intellect, and wherein established the said Yogī moves not from Truth on any account; (21)

यं लब्ध्वा चापरं लाभं मन्यते नाधिकं ततः।
यस्मिन्स्थितो न दुःखेन गुरुणापि विचाल्यते॥ २२॥

And having obtained which he does not reckon any other gain as greater than that, and established in which he is not shaken even by the heaviest of sorrows; (22)

तं विद्याद् दुःखसंयोगवियोगं योगसञ्ज्ञितम्।
स निश्चयेन योक्तव्यो योगोऽनिर्विण्णचेतसा॥ २३॥

That state, called Yoga, which is free from the contact of sorrow (in the form of transmigration), should be known. Nay, this Yoga should be resolutely practised with an unwearied mind. (23)

सङ्कल्पप्रभवान्कामांस्त्यक्त्वा सर्वानशेषतः।
मनसैवेन्द्रियग्रामं विनियम्य समन्ततः॥ २४॥

Completely renouncing all desires arising from Saṅkalpas (thoughts of the world), and fully restraining all the senses from all sides by the mind; (24)

शनैः शनैरुपरमेद्बुद्ध्या धृतिगृहीतया।
आत्मसंस्थं मनः कृत्वा न किञ्चिदपि चिन्तयेत्॥ २५॥

He should through gradual practice, attain tranquillity; and fixing the mind on God through reason controlled by steadfastness, he should not think of anything else. (25)

यतो यतो निश्चरति मनश्चञ्चलमस्थिरम्।
ततस्ततो नियम्यैतदात्मन्येव वशं नयेत्॥ २६॥

Drawing back the restless and fidgety mind from all those objects after which it runs, he should repeatedly fix it on God. (26)

प्रशान्तमनसं ह्येनं योगिनं सुखमुत्तमम्।
उपैति शान्तरजसं ब्रह्मभूतमकल्मषम्॥ २७॥

For, to the Yogī whose mind is perfectly serene, who is sinless, whose passion is subdued, and who is identified with Brahma, the embodiment of Truth, Knowledge and Bliss, supreme happiness comes as a matter of course. (27)

युञ्जन्नेवं सदात्मानं योगी विगतकल्मषः।
सुखेन ब्रह्मसंस्पर्शमत्यन्तं सुखमश्नुते॥ २८॥

The sinless Yogī, thus uniting his Self constantly with God, easily enjoys the eternal Bliss of oneness with Brahma. (28)

सर्वभूतस्थमात्मानं सर्वभूतानि चात्मनि।
ईक्षते योगयुक्तात्मा सर्वत्र समदर्शनः॥ २९॥

The Yogī who is united in identity with the all-pervading, infinite consciousness, whose vision everywhere is even, beholds the Self existing in all beings and all beings as assumed in the Self. (29)

यो मां पश्यति सर्वत्र सर्वं च मयि पश्यति।
तस्याहं न प्रणश्यामि स च मे न प्रणश्यति॥ ३०॥

He who sees Me (the Universal Self) present in all beings, and all beings existing within Me, he is never out of My sight, nor am I ever out of his sight. (30)

सर्वभूतस्थितं यो मां भजत्येकत्वमास्थितः।
सर्वथा वर्तमानोऽपि स योगी मयि वर्तते॥ ३१॥

The Yogī who is established in union with Me, and worships Me as residing in all beings as their very Self, whatever activities he performs, he performs them in Me. (31)

आत्मौपम्येन सर्वत्र समं पश्यति योऽर्जुन।
सुखं वा यदि वा दुःखं स योगी परमो मतः॥ ३२॥

Arjuna, he, who looks on all as one, on the analogy of his own Self, and looks upon the joy and sorrow of all equally–such a Yogī is deemed to be the highest of all. (32)

अर्जुन उवाच

योऽयं योगस्त्वया प्रोक्तः साम्येन मधुसूदन।
एतस्याहं न पश्यामि चञ्चलत्वात्स्थितिं स्थिराम्॥ ३३॥

Arjuna said : Kṛṣṇa, owing to restlessness of mind I do not perceive the stability of this Yoga in the form of equanimity, which You have just spoken of. (33)

चञ्चलं हि मनः कृष्ण प्रमाथि बलवद्दृढम्।
तस्याहं निग्रहं मन्ये वायोरिव सुदुष्करम्॥ ३४॥

For, Kṛṣṇa, the mind is very unsteady, turbulent, tenacious and powerful; therefore, I consider it as difficult to control as the wind. (34)

श्रीभगवानुवाच

असंशयं महाबाहो मनो दुर्निग्रहं चलम्।
अभ्यासेन तु कौन्तेय वैराग्येण च गृह्यते॥ ३५॥

Śrī Bhagavān said : The mind is restless no doubt, and difficult to curb, Arjuna; but it can be brought under control by repeated practice (of meditation) and by the exercise of dispassion, O son of Kuntī. (35)

असंयतात्मना योगो दुष्प्राप इति मे मतिः।
वश्यात्मना तु यतता शक्योऽवाप्तुमुपायतः॥ ३६॥

Yoga is difficult of achievement by one whose mind is not subdued by him; however, who has the mind under control, and is ceaselessly striving, it can be easily attained through practice. Such is My conviction. (36)

अर्जुन उवाच

अयतिः श्रद्धयोपेतो योगाच्चलितमानसः।
अप्राप्य योगसंसिद्धिं कां गतिं कृष्ण गच्छति॥ ३७॥

Arjuna said : Kṛṣṇa, what becomes of the aspirant who, though endowed with faith, has not been able to subdue his passions, and whose mind is, therefore, diverted from Yoga at the time of death, and who thus fails to reach perfection in Yoga (God-realization)? (37)

कच्चिन्नोभयविभ्रष्टश्छिन्नाभ्रमिव नश्यति।
अप्रतिष्ठो महाबाहो विमूढो ब्रह्मणः पथि॥ ३८॥

Kṛṣṇa, swerved from the path leading to God-realization and without anything to stand upon, is he not lost like the scattered cloud, deprived of both God-realization and heavenly enjoyment? (38)

एतन्मे संशयं कृष्ण छेत्तुमर्हस्यशेषतः।
त्वदन्यः संशयस्यास्य छेत्ता न ह्युपपद्यते॥ ३९॥

Kṛṣṇa, only You are capable to remove this doubt of mine completely; for none other than You can dispel this doubt. (39)

श्रीभगवानुवाच

पार्थ नैवेह नामुत्र विनाशस्तस्य विद्यते।
न हि कल्याणकृत्कश्चिद्दुर्गतिं तात गच्छति॥ ४०॥

Śrī Bhagavān said : Arjuna, there is no fall for him either here or hereafter. For, O My beloved, none who strives for self-redemption (i.e., God-realization) ever meets with evil destiny. (40)

प्राप्य पुण्यकृतां लोकानुषित्वा शाश्वतीः समाः।
शुचीनां श्रीमतां गेहे योगभ्रष्टोऽभिजायते॥ ४१॥

Such a person who has strayed from Yoga, obtains the higher worlds, (heaven etc.) to which men of meritorious deeds alone are entitled, and having resided there for innumerable years, takes birth of pious and prosperous parents. (41)

अथवा योगिनामेव कुले भवति धीमताम्।
एतद्धि दुर्लभतरं लोके जन्म यदीदृशम्॥ ४२॥

Or, if he is possessed of dispassion, then not attaining to those regions he is born in the family of enlightened Yogīs; but such a birth in this world is very difficult to obtain. (42)

तत्र तं बुद्धिसंयोगं लभते पौर्वदेहिकम्।
यतते च ततो भूयः संसिद्धौ कुरुनन्दन॥ ४३॥

Arjuna, he automatically regains in that birth the latencies of even-mindedness of his previous birth; and through that he strives harder than ever for perfection in the form of God-realization. (43)

पूर्वाभ्यासेन तेनैव ह्रियते ह्यवशोऽपि सः।
जिज्ञासुरपि योगस्य शब्दब्रह्मातिवर्तते॥ ४४॥

The other one who takes birth in a rich family, though under the sway of his senses, feels drawn towards God by force of the habit acquired in his previous birth; nay, even the seeker of Yoga (in the form of even-mindedness) transcends the fruit of actions performed with some interested motive as laid down in the Vedas. (44)

प्रयत्नाद्यतमानस्तु योगी संशुद्धकिल्बिषः।
अनेकजन्मसंसिद्धस्ततो याति परां गतिम्॥ ४५॥

The Yogī, however, who diligently takes up the practice, attains perfection in this very life with the help of latencies of many births, and being thoroughly purged of sin, forthwith reaches the supreme state. (45)

तपस्विभ्योऽधिको योगी ज्ञानिभ्योऽपि मतोऽधिकः।
कर्मिभ्यश्चाधिको योगी तस्माद्योगी भवार्जुन॥ ४६॥

The Yogī is superior to the ascetics; he is regarded superior even to those versed in sacred lore. The Yogī is also superior to those who perform action with some interested motive. Therefore, Arjuna, do become a Yogī. (46)

योगिनामपि सर्वेषां मद्गतेनान्तरात्मना।
श्रद्धावान्भजते यो मां स मे युक्ततमो मतः॥ ४७॥

Of all Yogīs, again, he who devoutly worships Me with his mind focussed on Me is considered by Me to be the best Yogī. (47)

ॐ तत्सदिति श्रीमद्भगवद्गीतासूपनिषत्सु ब्रह्मविद्यायां
योगशास्त्रे श्रीकृष्णार्जुनसंवादे आत्मसंयमयोगो
नाम षष्ठोऽध्यायः॥ ६॥

Thus, in the Upaniṣad sung by the Lord, the Science of Brahma, the scripture of Yoga, the dialogue between Śrī Kṛṣṇa and Arjuna, ends the sixth chapter entitled "The Yoga of Self-control."

Chapter VII

श्रीभगवानुवाच

मय्यासक्तमनाः पार्थ योगं युञ्जन्मदाश्रयः।
असंशयं समग्रं मां यथा ज्ञास्यसि तच्छृणु॥ १॥

Śrī Bhagavān said : Arjuna, now listen how with the mind attached to Me (through exclusive love) and practising Yoga with absolute dependence on Me, you will know Me, the repository of all power, strength and glory and other attributes, the Universal soul, in entirety and without any shadow of doubt. (1)

ज्ञानं तेऽहं सविज्ञानमिदं वक्ष्याम्यशेषतः।
यज्ज्ञात्वा नेह भूयोऽन्यज्ज्ञातव्यमवशिष्यते॥ २॥

I shall unfold to you in its entirety this wisdom (Knowledge of God in His absolute formless aspect) along with the Knowledge of the qualified aspect of God (both with form and without form), having known which nothing else remains yet to be known in this world. (2)

मनुष्याणां सहस्रेषु कश्चिद्यतति सिद्धये।
यततामपि सिद्धानां कश्चिन्मां वेत्ति तत्त्वतः॥ ३॥

Hardly one among thousands of men strives to realize Me; of those striving Yogīs, again, some rare one, devoting himself exclusively to Me, knows Me in reality. (3)

भूमिरापोऽनलो वायुः खं मनो बुद्धिरेव च।
अहङ्कार इतीयं मे भिन्ना प्रकृतिरष्टधा॥ ४॥
अपरेयमितस्त्वन्यां प्रकृतिं विद्धि मे पराम्।
जीवभूतां महाबाहो ययेदं धार्यते जगत्॥ ५॥

Earth, water, fire, air, ether, mind, reason and also ego—these constitute My nature divided into eight parts. This indeed is My lower (material) nature; the other than this, by which the whole universe is sustained, know it to be My higher (or spiritual) nature in the form of Jīva (the life-principle), O Arjuna. (4-5)

एतद्योनीनि भूतानि सर्वाणीत्युपधारय।
अहं कृत्स्नस्य जगतः प्रभवः प्रलयस्तथा॥ ६॥

Arjuna, know that all beings have evolved from this twofold Prakṛti, and that I am the source of the entire creation, and into Me again it dissolves. (6)

मत्तः परतरं नान्यत्किञ्चिदस्ति धनञ्जय।
मयि सर्वमिदं प्रोतं सूत्रे मणिगणा इव॥ ७॥

There is nothing else besides Me, Arjuna. Like clusters of yarn-beads formed by knots on a thread, all this is threaded on Me. (7)

रसोऽहमप्सु कौन्तेय प्रभास्मि शशिसूर्ययोः।
प्रणवः सर्ववेदेषु शब्दः खे पौरुषं नृषु॥ ८॥

Arjuna, I am the sapidity in water and the radiance in the moon and the sun; I am the sacred syllable OṀ in all the Vedas, the sound in ether, and virility in men. (8)

पुण्यो गन्धः पृथिव्यां च तेजश्चास्मि विभावसौ।
जीवनं सर्वभूतेषु तपश्चास्मि तपस्विषु॥ ९ ॥

I am the pure odour (the subtle principle of smell) in the earth and the brightness in fire; nay, I am the life in all beings and austerity in the ascetics. (9)

बीजं मां सर्वभूतानां विद्धि पार्थ सनातनम्।
बुद्धिर्बुद्धिमतामस्मि तेजस्तेजस्विनामहम्॥ १० ॥

Arjuna, know Me the eternal seed of all beings. I am the intelligence of the intelligent; the glory of the glorious am I. (10)

बलं बलवतां चाहं कामरागविवर्जितम्।
धर्माविरुद्धो भूतेषु कामोऽस्मि भरतर्षभ॥ ११ ॥

Arjuna, of the mighty I am the might, free from passion and desire; in beings I am the sexual desire not conflicting with virtue or scriptural injunctions. (11)

ये चैव सात्त्विका भावा राजसास्तामसाश्च ये।
मत्त एवेति तान्विद्धि न त्वहं तेषु ते मयि॥ १२ ॥

Whatever other entities there are, born of Sattva (the quality of goodness), and those that are born of Rajas (the principle of activity) and Tamas (the principle of inertia), know them all as evolved from Me alone. In reality, however, neither do I exist in them, nor do they in Me. (12)

त्रिभिर्गुणमयैर्भावैरेभिः सर्वमिदं जगत्।
मोहितं नाभिजानाति मामेभ्यः परमव्ययम्॥ १३॥

The whole of this creation is deluded by these objects evolved from the three modes of Prakṛti—Sattva, Rajas and Tamas; that is why the world fails to recognize Me, standing apart from these, the Imperishable. (13)

दैवी ह्येषा गुणमयी मम माया दुरत्यया।
मामेव ये प्रपद्यन्ते मायामेतां तरन्ति ते॥ १४॥

For, this most wonderful Māyā (veil) of Mine, consisting of the three Guṇas (modes of Nature), is extremely difficult to breakthrough; those, however, who constantly adore Me alone, are able to cross it. (14)

न मां दुष्कृतिनो मूढाः प्रपद्यन्ते नराधमाः।
माययापहृतज्ञाना आसुरं भावमाश्रिताः॥ १५॥

Those whose wisdom has been carried away by Māyā, and are of demoniac nature, such foolish and vile men of evil deeds do not adore Me. (15)

चतुर्विधा भजन्ते मां जनाः सुकृतिनोऽर्जुन।
आर्तो जिज्ञासुरर्थार्थी ज्ञानी च भरतर्षभ॥ १६॥

Four types of devotees of noble deeds worship Me, Arjuna, the seeker after worldly possessions, the afflicted, the seeker for knowledge, and the man of wisdom, O best of Bharatas. (16)

तेषां ज्ञानी नित्ययुक्त एकभक्तिर्विशिष्यते।
प्रियो हि ज्ञानिनोऽत्यर्थमहं स च मम प्रियः॥ १७॥

Of these, the best is the man of wisdom, ever established in identity with Me and possessed of exclusive devotion. For, I am extremely dear to the wise man who knows Me in reality, and he is extremely dear to Me. (17)

उदाराः सर्व एवैते ज्ञानी त्वात्मैव मे मतम्।
आस्थितः स हि युक्तात्मा मामेवानुत्तमां गतिम्॥ १८॥

Indeed, all these are noble, but the man of wisdom is My very self; such is My view. For such a devotee, who has his mind and intellect merged in Me, is firmly established in Me alone as the highest goal. (18)

बहूनां जन्मनामन्ते ज्ञानवान्मां प्रपद्यते।
वासुदेवः सर्वमिति स महात्मा सुदुर्लभः॥ १९॥

In the very last of all births the enlightened person worships Me by realizing that all this is God. Such a great soul is very rare indeed.(19)

कामैस्तैस्तैर्हृतज्ञानाः प्रपद्यन्तेऽन्यदेवताः।
तं तं नियममास्थाय प्रकृत्या नियताः स्वया॥ २०॥

Those whose wisdom has been carried away by various desires, being prompted by their own nature, worship other deities, adopting norms relating to each. (20)

यो यो यां यां तनुं भक्तः श्रद्धयार्चितुमिच्छति।
तस्य तस्याचलां श्रद्धां तामेव विदधाम्यहम्॥ २१॥

Whatever celestial form a devotee (craving for some worldly object) chooses to worship with reverence, I stabilize the faith of that particular devotee in that very form. (21)

स तया श्रद्धया युक्तस्तस्याराधनमीहते।
लभते च ततः कामान्मयैव विहितान्हि तान्॥ २२॥

Endowed with such faith, he worships that particular deity and obtains through that deity without doubt his desired enjoyments as verily ordained by Me. (22)

अन्तवत्तु फलं तेषां तद्भवत्यल्पमेधसाम्।
देवान्देवयजो यान्ति मद्भक्ता यान्ति मामपि॥ २३॥

The fruit gained by these people of small understanding, however, is perishable. The worshippers of gods attain the gods; whereas My devotees, howsoever they worship Me, eventually come to Me and Me alone. (23)

अव्यक्तं व्यक्तिमापन्नं मन्यन्ते मामबुद्धयः।
परं भावमजानन्तो ममाव्ययमनुत्तमम्॥ २४॥

Not knowing My supreme nature, unsurpassable and undecaying, the ignorant persons regard Me, who am the Supreme Spirit beyond the reach of mind and senses, and the embodiment of Truth, Knowledge and Bliss, to have assumed a finite form through birth as an ordinary human being. (24)

नाहं प्रकाशः सर्वस्य योगमायासमावृतः।
मूढोऽयं नाभिजानाति लोको मामजमव्ययम्॥ २५॥

Veiled by My Yogamāyā, My divine potency, I am not manifest to all. Hence these ignorant folk fail to recognize Me, the birthless and imperishable Supreme Deity i.e., consider Me as subject to birth and death. (25)

वेदाहं समतीतानि वर्तमानानि चार्जुन।
भविष्याणि च भूतानि मां तु वेद न कश्चन॥ २६॥

Arjuna, I know all beings, past as well as present, nay, even those that are yet to come; but none, devoid of faith and devotion, knows Me. (26)

इच्छाद्वेषसमुत्थेन द्वन्द्वमोहेन भारत।
सर्वभूतानि सम्मोहं सर्गे यान्ति परन्तप॥ २७॥

O valiant Arjuna, through delusion in the form of pairs of opposites (such as pleasure and pain etc.,) born of desire and aversion, all living creatures in this world are falling a prey to infatuation. (27)

येषां त्वन्तगतं पापं जनानां पुण्यकर्मणाम्।
ते द्वन्द्वमोहनिर्मुक्ता भजन्ते मां दृढव्रताः॥ २८॥

But those men of virtuous deeds, whose sins have come to an end, being freed from delusion in the form of pairs of opposites born of attraction and repulsion, worship Me with a firm resolve in every way. (28)

जरामरणमोक्षाय मामाश्रित्य यतन्ति ये।
ते ब्रह्म तद्विदुः कृत्स्नमध्यात्मं कर्म चाखिलम्॥ २९॥
साधिभूताधिदैवं मां साधियज्ञं च ये विदुः।
प्रयाणकालेऽपि च मां ते विदुर्युक्तचेतसः॥ ३०॥

They who, having taken refuge in Me, strive for deliverance from old age and death, know Brahma (the Absolute), the whole Adhyātma (the totality of Jīvas or embodied souls), and the entire field of Karma (action) as well as My integral being, comprising Adhibhūta (the field of Matter), Adhidaiva (Brahmā) and Adhiyajña (the unmanifest Divinity dwelling in the heart of all beings as their witness). And they who, possessed of a steadfast mind, know thus even at the hour of death, they too know Me alone. (29-30)

ॐ तत्सदिति श्रीमद्भगवद्गीतासूपनिषत्सु ब्रह्मविद्यायां
योगशास्त्रे श्रीकृष्णार्जुनसंवादे ज्ञानविज्ञानयोगो
नाम सप्तमोऽध्यायः॥ ७॥

Thus, in the Upaniṣad sung by the Lord, the Science of Brahma, the scripture of Yoga, the dialogue between Śrī Kṛṣṇa and Arjuna, ends the seventh chapter entitled "The Yoga of Jñāna (Knowledge of Nirguṇa Brahma) and Vijñāna (Knowledge of Manifest Divinity)."

Chapter VIII

अर्जुन उवाच

किं तद्ब्रह्म किमध्यात्मं किं कर्म पुरुषोत्तम।
अधिभूतं च किं प्रोक्तमधिदैवं किमुच्यते॥ १॥

Arjuna said : Kṛṣṇa, what is that Brahma (Absolute), what is Adhyātma (Spirit), and what is Karma (Action)? What is called Adhibhūta (Matter) and what is termed as Adhidaiva (Divine Intelligence)? (1)

अधियज्ञः कथं कोऽत्र देहेऽस्मिन्मधुसूदन।
प्रयाणकाले च कथं ज्ञेयोऽसि नियतात्मभिः॥ २॥

Kṛṣṇa, who is Adhiyajña here and how does he dwell in the body? And how are You to be realized at the time of death by those of steadfast mind? (2)

श्रीभगवानुवाच

अक्षरं ब्रह्म परमं स्वभावोऽध्यात्ममुच्यते।
भूतभावोद्भवकरो विसर्गः कर्मसञ्ज्ञितः॥ ३॥

Śrī Bhagavān said:The supreme Indestructible is Brahma, one's own Self (the individual soul) is called Adhyātma; and the Primal resolve of God, (Visarga), which brings forth the existence of beings, is called Karma (Action). (3)

अधिभूतं क्षरो भावः पुरुषश्चाधिदैवतम्।
अधियज्ञोऽहमेवात्र देहे देहभृतां वर॥ ४॥

All perishable objects are Adhibhūta; the shining Puruṣa (Brahmā) is Adhidaiva; and in this body I Myself, dwelling as the inner witness, am Adhiyajña, O Arjuna! (4)

अन्तकाले च मामेव स्मरन्मुक्त्वा कलेवरम्।
यः प्रयाति स मद्भावं याति नास्त्यत्र संशयः॥ ५॥

He who departs from the body, thinking of Me alone even at the time of death, attains My state; there is no doubt about it. (5)

यं यं वापि स्मरन्भावं त्यजत्यन्ते कलेवरम्।
तं तमेवैति कौन्तेय सदा तद्भावभावितः॥ ६॥

Arjuna, thinking of whatever entity one leaves the body at the time of death, that and that alone one attains, being ever absorbed in its thought. (6)

तस्मात्सर्वेषु कालेषु मामनुस्मर युध्य च।
मय्यर्पितमनोबुद्धिर्मामेवैष्यस्यसंशयम्॥ ७॥

Therefore, Arjuna, think of Me at all times and fight. With mind and reason thus set on Me, you will doubtless come to Me. (7)

अभ्यासयोगयुक्तेन चेतसा नान्यगामिना।
परमं पुरुषं दिव्यं याति पार्थानुचिन्तयन्॥ ८॥

Arjuna, he who with his mind disciplined through Yoga in the form of practice of meditation and thinking of nothing else, is constantly engaged in contemplation of God attains the supremely effulgent Divine Puruṣa (God). (8)

कविं पुराणमनुशासितार-
मणोरणीयांसमनुस्मरेद्यः ।
सर्वस्य धातारमचिन्त्यरूप-
मादित्यवर्णं तमसः परस्तात्॥ ९ ॥

He who contemplates on the all-knowing, ageless Being, the Ruler of all, subtler than the subtle, the universal sustainer, possessing a form beyond human conception, effulgent like the sun and far beyond the darkness of ignorance. (9)

प्रयाणकाले मनसाचलेन
भक्त्या युक्तो योगबलेन चैव।
भ्रुवोर्मध्ये प्राणमावेश्य सम्यक्-
स तं परं पुरुषमुपैति दिव्यम्॥ १०॥

Having by the power of Yoga firmly held the life-breath in the space between the two eyebrows even at the time of death, and then contemplating on God with a steadfast mind, full of devotion, he reaches verily that supreme divine Puruṣa (God). (10)

यदक्षरं वेदविदो वदन्ति
विशन्ति यद्यतयो वीतरागाः।
यदिच्छन्तो ब्रह्मचर्यं चरन्ति
तत्ते पदं सङ्ग्रहेण प्रवक्ष्ये॥ ११॥

I shall tell you briefly about that Supreme goal

(viz., God, who is an embodiment of Truth, Knowledge and Bliss), which the knowers of the Veda term as the Indestructible, which striving recluses, free from passion, merge into, and desiring which the celibates practise Brahmacarya. (11)

सर्वद्वाराणि संयम्य मनो हृदि निरुध्य च।
मूर्ध्न्याधायात्मनः प्राणमास्थितो योगधारणाम्॥ १२॥
ओमित्येकाक्षरं ब्रह्म व्याहरन्मामनुस्मरन्।
यः प्रयाति त्यजन्देहं स याति परमां गतिम्॥ १३॥

Having controlled all the senses, and firmly holding the mind in the heart, and then drawing the life-breath to the head, and thus remaining steadfast in Yogic concentration on God, he who leaves the body and departs uttering the one Indestructible Brahma, OM, and dwelling on Me in My absolute aspect, reaches the supreme goal. (12-13)

अनन्यचेताः सततं यो मां स्मरति नित्यशः।
तस्याहं सुलभः पार्थ नित्ययुक्तस्य योगिनः॥ १४॥

Arjuna, whosoever always and constantly thinks of Me with undivided mind, to that Yogī ever absorbed in Me I am easily attainable. (14)

मामुपेत्य पुनर्जन्म दुःखालयमशाश्वतम्।
नाप्नुवन्ति महात्मानः संसिद्धिं परमां गताः॥ १५॥

Great souls, who have attained the highest perfection, having come to Me, are no more subject to transitory rebirth, which is the abode of sorrow, and transient by nature. (15)

आब्रह्मभुवनाल्लोकाः पुनरावर्तिनोऽर्जुन।
मामुपेत्य तु कौन्तेय पुनर्जन्म न विद्यते॥ १६॥

Arjuna, all the worlds from Brahmaloka (the heavenly realm of the Creator, Brahmā) downwards are liable to birth and rebirth. But, O son of Kuntī, on attaining Me there is no rebirth (For, while I am beyond Time, regions like Brahmaloka, being conditioned by time, are transitory). (16)

सहस्रयुगपर्यन्तमहर्यद्ब्रह्मणो विदुः।
रात्रिं युगसहस्रान्तां तेऽहोरात्रविदो जनाः॥ १७॥

Those Yogīs, who know from realization Brahmā's day as covering a thousand Mahāyugas, and so his night as extending to another thousand Mahāyugas, know the reality about Time. (17)

अव्यक्ताद्व्यक्तयः सर्वाः प्रभवन्त्यहरागमे।
रात्र्यागमे प्रलीयन्ते तत्रैवाव्यक्तसञ्ज्ञके॥ १८॥

All embodied beings emanate from the Unmanifest (i.e., Brahmā's subtle body) at the coming of the cosmic day; at the cosmic nightfall they merge into the same subtle body of Brahmā, known as the Unmanifest. (18)

भूतग्रामः स एवायं भूत्वा भूत्वा प्रलीयते।
रात्र्यागमेऽवशः पार्थ प्रभवत्यहरागमे॥ १९॥

Arjuna, this multitude of beings, being born again and again, is dissolved under compulsion of its nature at the coming of the cosmic night, and rises again at the commencement of the cosmic day. (19)

परस्तस्मात्तु भावोऽन्योऽव्यक्तोऽव्यक्तात्सनातनः।
यः स सर्वेषु भूतेषु नश्यत्सु न विनश्यति॥ २०॥

Far beyond even this unmanifest, there is yet another unmanifest Existence, that Supreme Divine Person, who does not perish even though all beings perish. (20)

अव्यक्तोऽक्षर इत्युक्तस्तमाहुः परमां गतिम्।
यं प्राप्य न निवर्तन्ते तद्धाम परमं मम॥ २१॥

The same unmanifest which has been spoken of as the Indestructible, is also called the supreme goal; that again is My supreme Abode, attaining which they return not to this mortal world.(21)

पुरुषः स परः पार्थ भक्त्या लभ्यस्त्वनन्यया।
यस्यान्तःस्थानि भूतानि येन सर्वमिदं ततम्॥ २२॥

Arjuna, that eternal unmanifest supreme Puruṣa in whom all beings reside and by whom all this is pervaded, is attainable only through exclusive Devotion. (22)

यत्र काले त्वनावृत्तिमावृत्तिं चैव योगिनः।
प्रयाता यान्ति तं कालं वक्ष्यामि भरतर्षभ॥ २३॥

Arjuna, I shall now tell you the time (path) departing when Yogīs do not return, and also the time (path) departing when they do return. (23)

अग्निर्ज्योतिरहः शुक्लः षण्मासा उत्तरायणम्।
तत्र प्रयाता गच्छन्ति ब्रह्म ब्रह्मविदो जनाः॥ २४॥

(Of the two paths) the one is that in which are stationed the all-effulgent fire-god and the deities presiding over daylight, the bright fortnight, and the six months of the northward course of the sun respectively; proceeding along it after death Yogīs, who have known Brahma, being successively led by the above gods, finally reach Brahma. (24)

धूमो रात्रिस्तथा कृष्णः षण्मासा दक्षिणायनम्।
तत्र चान्द्रमसं ज्योतिर्योगी प्राप्य निवर्तते॥ २५॥

The other path is that wherein are stationed the gods presiding over smoke, night, the dark fortnight, and the six months of the southward course of the sun; the Yogī (devoted to action with an interested motive) taking to this path after death is led by the above gods, one after another, and attaining the lustre of the moon (and enjoying the fruit of his meritorious deeds in heaven) returns to this mortal world. (25)

शुक्लकृष्णे गती ह्येते जगतः शाश्वते मते।
एकया यात्यनावृत्तिमन्ययावर्तते पुनः॥ २६॥

For these two paths of the world, the bright and the dark, are considered to be eternal. Proceeding by one of them, one reaches the supreme state from which there is no return; and proceeding by the other, one returns to the mortal world, i.e., becomes subject to birth and death once more. (26)

नैते सृती पार्थ जानन्योगी मुह्यति कश्चन।
तस्मात्सर्वेषु कालेषु योगयुक्तो भवार्जुन॥ २७॥

Knowing thus the secret of these two paths, O son of Kuntī, no Yogī gets deluded. Therefore, Arjuna, at all times be steadfast in Yoga in the form of equanimity (i.e., strive constantly for My realization). (27)

वेदेषु यज्ञेषु तपःसु चैव
दानेषु यत्पुण्यफलं प्रदिष्टम्।
अत्येति तत्सर्वमिदं विदित्वा
योगी परं स्थानमुपैति चाद्यम्॥ २८॥

The Yogī, realizing this profound truth, doubtless transcends all the rewards enumerated for the study of the Vedas as well as for the performance of sacrifices, austerities and charities, and attains the supreme and primal state. (28)

ॐ तत्सदिति श्रीमद्भगवद्गीतासूपनिषत्सु ब्रह्मविद्यायां
योगशास्त्रे श्रीकृष्णार्जुनसंवादे अक्षरब्रह्मयोगो
नामाष्टमोऽध्यायः॥ ८॥

Thus, in the Upaniṣad sung by the Lord, the Science of Brahma, the scripture of Yoga, the dialogue between Śrī Kṛṣṇa and Arjuna, ends the eighth chapter entitled "The Yoga of the Indestructible Brahma."

Chapter IX

श्रीभगवानुवाच

इदं तु ते गुह्यतमं प्रवक्ष्याम्यनसूयवे।
ज्ञानं विज्ञानसहितं यज्ज्ञात्वा मोक्ष्यसेऽशुभात्॥ १॥

Śrī Bhagavān said : To you, who are devoid of the carping spirit, I shall now unfold the most secret knowledge of Nirguṇa Brahma along with the knowledge of manifest Divinity, knowing which you shall be free from the evil of worldly existence. (1)

राजविद्या राजगुह्यं पवित्रमिदमुत्तमम्।
प्रत्यक्षावगमं धर्म्यं सुसुखं कर्तुमव्ययम्॥ २॥

This knowledge (of both the Nirguṇa and Saguṇa aspects of Divinity) is a sovereign science, a sovereign secret, supremely holy, most excellent, directly enjoyable, attended with virtue, very easy to practise and imperishable. (2)

अश्रद्दधानाः पुरुषा धर्मस्यास्य परन्तप।
अप्राप्य मां निवर्तन्ते मृत्युसंसारवर्त्मनि॥ ३॥

Arjuna, people having no faith in this Dharma, failing to reach Me, continue to revolve in the path of the world of birth and death. (3)

मया ततमिदं सर्वं जगदव्यक्तमूर्तिना।
मत्स्थानि सर्वभूतानि न चाहं तेष्ववस्थितः॥ ४॥

The whole of this universe is permeated by Me as unmanifest Divinity, like ice by water and all beings dwell on the idea within Me. But, really speaking, I am not present in them. (4)

न च मत्स्थानि भूतानि पश्य मे योगमैश्वरम्।
भूतभृन्न च भूतस्थो ममात्मा भूतभावनः॥ ५॥

Nay, all those beings abide not in Me; but behold the wonderful power of My divine Yoga; though the Sustainer and Creator of beings, Myself in reality dwell not in those beings. (5)

यथाकाशस्थितो नित्यं वायुः सर्वत्रगो महान्।
तथा सर्वाणि भूतानि मत्स्थानीत्युपधारय॥ ६॥

Just as the extensive air, which is moving everywhere, (being born of ether) ever remains in ether, likewise, know that all beings, who have originated from My Saṅkalpa, abide in Me. (6)

सर्वभूतानि कौन्तेय प्रकृतिं यान्ति मामिकाम्।
कल्पक्षये पुनस्तानि कल्पादौ विसृजाम्यहम्॥ ७॥

Arjuna, during the Final Dissolution all beings enter My Prakṛti (the prime cause), and at the beginning of creation, I send them forth again. (7)

प्रकृतिं स्वामवष्टभ्य विसृजामि पुनः पुनः।
भूतग्राममिमं कृत्स्नमवशं प्रकृतेर्वशात्॥ ८॥

Wielding My Nature I procreate again and again, according to their respective Karmas, all this multitude of beings subject to the sway of their own nature. (8)

न च मां तानि कर्माणि निबध्नन्ति धनञ्जय।
उदासीनवदासीनमसक्तं तेषु कर्मसु॥ ९ ॥

Arjuna, those actions, however, do not bind Me, unattached as I am to such actions, and standing apart as it were. (9)

मयाध्यक्षेण प्रकृतिः सूयते सचराचरम्।
हेतुनानेन कौन्तेय जगद्विपरिवर्तते॥ १० ॥

Arjuna, under My aegis, Nature brings forth the whole creation, consisting of both sentient and insentient beings; it is due to this cause that the wheel of Saṁsāra is going round. (10)

अवजानन्ति मां मूढा मानुषीं तनुमाश्रितम्।
परं भावमजानन्तो मम भूतमहेश्वरम्॥ ११ ॥

Not Knowing My supreme nature, fools deride Me, the Overlord of the entire creation, who have assumed the human form. That is to say, they take Me, who have appeared in human form through My 'Yogamāyā' for deliverance of the world, as an ordinary mortal. (11)

मोघाशा मोघकर्माणो मोघज्ञाना विचेतसः।
राक्षसीमासुरीं चैव प्रकृतिं मोहिनीं श्रिताः॥ १२ ॥

Those bewildered persons with vain hopes, futile actions and fruitless knowledge, have embraced a fiendish, demoniacal and delusive nature. (12)

महात्मानस्तु मां पार्थ दैवीं प्रकृतिमाश्रिताः।
भजन्त्यनन्यमनसो ज्ञात्वा भूतादिमव्ययम्॥ १३॥

On the other hand, Arjuna, great souls who have adopted the divine nature, knowing Me as the prime source of all beings and the imperishable eternal, worship Me constantly with one-pointedness of mind. (13)

सततं कीर्तयन्तो मां यतन्तश्च दृढव्रताः।
नमस्यन्तश्च मां भक्त्या नित्ययुक्ता उपासते॥ १४॥

Constantly chanting My names and glories and striving for My realization, and bowing again and again to Me, those devotees of firm resolve, ever united with me through meditation, worship Me with single-minded devotion. (14)

ज्ञानयज्ञेन चाप्यन्ये यजन्तो मामुपासते।
एकत्वेन पृथक्त्वेन बहुधा विश्वतोमुखम्॥ १५॥

Others, who follow the path of Knowledge, betake themselves to Me through Yajña of Knowledge, worshipping Me in My absolute, formless aspect as one with themselves; while still others worship Me in My Universal Form in many ways, taking Me to be diverse in manifold celestial forms. (15)

अहं क्रतुरहं यज्ञः स्वधाहमहमौषधम्।
मन्त्रोऽहमहमेवाज्यमहमग्निरहं हुतम्॥ १६॥

I am the Vedic ritual, I am the sacrifice, I am the offering to the departed; I am the herbage and foodgrains; I am the sacred mantra, I am the clarified butter, I am the sacred fire, and I am verily the act of offering oblations into the fire. (16)

पिताहमस्य जगतो माता धाता पितामहः।
वेद्यं पवित्रमोङ्कार ऋक्साम यजुरेव च॥ १७॥

I am the sustainer and ruler of this universe, its father, mother and grandfather, the one worth knowing, the purifier, the sacred syllable OṀ, and the three Vedas—Ṛk, Yajuṣ and Sāma. (17)

गतिर्भर्ता प्रभुः साक्षी निवासः शरणं सुहृत्।
प्रभवः प्रलयः स्थानं निधानं बीजमव्ययम्॥ १८॥

I am the supreme goal, sustainer, lord, witness, abode, refuge, well-wisher seeking no return, origin and end, resting-place, store-house to which all beings return at the time of universal destruction, and the imperishable seed. (18)

तपाम्यहमहं वर्षं निगृह्णाम्युत्सृजामि च।
अमृतं चैव मृत्युश्च सदसच्चाहमर्जुन॥ १९॥

I radiate heat as the sun, and hold back as well as send forth showers, Arjuna. I am immortality as well as death; even so, I am being and also non-being. (19)

त्रैविद्या मां सोमपाः पूतपापा-
यज्ञैरिष्ट्वा स्वर्गतिं प्रार्थयन्ते।
ते पुण्यमासाद्य सुरेन्द्रलोक-
मश्नन्ति दिव्यान्दिवि देवभोगान्॥ २०॥

Those who perform action with some interested motive as laid down in these three Vedas and drink the sap of the Soma plant, and have thus been purged of sin, worshipping Me through sacrifices, seek access to heaven; attaining Indra's paradise as the result of their virtuous deeds, they enjoy the celestial pleasures of gods in heaven. (20)

ते तं भुक्त्वा स्वर्गलोकं विशालं-
क्षीणे पुण्ये मर्त्यलोकं विशन्ति।
एवं त्रयीधर्ममनुप्रपन्ना-
गतागतं कामकामा लभन्ते॥ २१॥

Having enjoyed the extensive heaven-world, they return to this world of mortals on the stock of their merits being exhausted. Thus devoted to the ritual with interested motive, recommended by the three Vedas as the means of attaining heavenly bliss, and seeking worldly enjoyments, they repeatedly come and go (i.e., ascend to heaven by virtue of their merits and return to earth when their fruit has been enjoyed). (21)

अनन्याश्चिन्तयन्तो मां ये जनाः पर्युपासते।
तेषां नित्याभियुक्तानां योगक्षेमं वहाम्यहम्॥ २२॥

The devotees, however, who loving no one else constantly think of Me, and worship Me in a disinterested spirit, to those ever united in thought with Me, I bring full security and personally attend to their needs. (22)

येऽप्यन्यदेवता भक्ता यजन्ते श्रद्धयान्विताः।
तेऽपि मामेव कौन्तेय यजन्त्यविधिपूर्वकम्॥ २३॥

Arjuna, even those devotees who, endowed with

faith, worship other gods (with some interested motive) worship Me alone, though with a mistaken approach. (23)

अहं हि सर्वयज्ञानां भोक्ता च प्रभुरेव च।
न तु मामभिजानन्ति तत्त्वेनातश्च्यवन्ति ते॥ २४॥

For, I am the enjoyer and also the lord of all sacrifices; but they who do not know Me in reality as the Supreme Deity, they fall i.e., return to life on earth. (24)

यान्ति देवव्रता देवान्पितॄन्यान्ति पितृव्रताः।
भूतानि यान्ति भूतेज्या यान्ति मद्याजिनोऽपि माम्॥ २५॥

Those who are votaries of gods, go to gods, those who are votaries of manes, reach the manes; those who adore the spirits, reach the spirits and those who worship Me, come to Me alone. That is why My devotees are no longer subject to birth and death. (25)

पत्रं पुष्पं फलं तोयं यो मे भक्त्या प्रयच्छति।
तदहं भक्त्युपहृतमश्नामि प्रयतात्मनः॥ २६॥

Whosoever offers Me with love a leaf, a flower, a fruit or water, I, appear in person before that selfless devotee of sinless mind, and delightfully partake of that article offered by him with love. (26)

यत्करोषि यदश्नासि यज्जुहोषि ददासि यत्।
यत्तपस्यसि कौन्तेय तत्कुरुष्व मदर्पणम्॥ २७॥

Arjuna, whatever you do, whatever you eat, whatever you offer as oblation to the sacred fire, whatever you bestow as a gift, whatever you do by way of penance, offer all that to Me. (27)

शुभाशुभफलैरेवं मोक्ष्यसे कर्मबन्धनैः।
सन्न्यासयोगयुक्तात्मा विमुक्तो मामुपैष्यसि॥ २८॥

With your mind thus established in the Yoga of renunciation (offering of all actions to Me), you will be freed from the bondage of action in the form of good and evil results; thus freed from them, you will attain Me. (28)

समोऽहं सर्वभूतेषु न मे द्वेष्योऽस्ति न प्रियः।
ये भजन्ति तु मां भक्त्या मयि ते तेषु चाप्यहम्॥ २९॥

I am equally present in all beings; there is none hateful or dear to Me. They, however, who devoutly worship Me abide in Me; and I too stand revealed to them. (29)

अपि चेत्सुदुराचारो भजते मामनन्यभाक्।
साधुरेव स मन्तव्यः सम्यग्व्यवसितो हि सः॥ ३०॥

Even if the vilest sinner worships Me with exclusive devotion, he should be regarded a saint; for, he has rightly resolved. (He is positive in his belief that there is nothing like devoted worship of God). (30)

क्षिप्रं भवति धर्मात्मा शश्वच्छान्तिं निगच्छति।
कौन्तेय प्रतिजानीहि न मे भक्तः प्रणश्यति॥ ३१॥

Speedily he becomes virtuous and attains abiding peace. Know it for certain, Arjuna, that My devotee never perishes. (31)

मां हि पार्थ व्यपाश्रित्य येऽपि स्युः पापयोनयः।
स्त्रियो वैश्यास्तथा शूद्रास्तेऽपि यान्ति परां गतिम्॥ ३२॥

Arjuna, women, Vaiśyas (members of the trading and agriculturist classes), Śūdras (those belonging to the labour and artisan classes), as well as those of impious birth (such as the pariah), whoever they may be, taking refuge in Me, they too attain the supreme goal. (32)

किं पुनर्ब्राह्मणाः पुण्या भक्ता राजर्षयस्तथा।
अनित्यमसुखं लोकमिमं प्राप्य भजस्व माम्॥ ३३॥

How much more, then, if they be holy Brāhmaṇas and royal sages devoted to Me! Therefore, having obtained this joyless and transient human life, constantly worship Me. (33)

मन्मना भव मद्भक्तो मद्याजी मां नमस्कुरु।
मामेवैष्यसि युक्त्वैवमात्मानं मत्परायणः॥ ३४॥

Fix your mind on Me, be devoted to Me, worship Me and make obeisance to Me; thus linking yourself with Me and entirely depending on Me, you shall come to Me. (34)

ॐ तत्सदिति श्रीमद्भगवद्गीतासूपनिषत्सु ब्रह्मविद्यायां
योगशास्त्रे श्रीकृष्णार्जुनसंवादे राजविद्याराज-
गुह्ययोगो नाम नवमोऽध्यायः॥ ९॥

Thus, in the Upaniṣad sung by the Lord, the Science of Brahma, the scripture of Yoga, the dialogue between Śrī Kṛṣṇa and Arjuna, ends the ninth chapter entitled "The Yoga of Sovereign Science and the Sovereign Secret."

Chapter X

श्रीभगवानुवाच

भूय एव महाबाहो शृणु मे परमं वचः।
यत्तेऽहं प्रीयमाणाय वक्ष्यामि हितकाम्यया॥ १॥

Śrī Bhagavān said : Arjuna, hear once again My supreme word, which I shall speak to you, who are so loving, out of solicitude for your welfare. (1)

न मे विदुः सुरगणाः प्रभवं न महर्षयः।
अहमादिर्हि देवानां महर्षीणां च सर्वशः॥ २॥

Neither gods nor the great sages know the secret of My birth (i.e., My manifestation in human or other forms out of mere sport); for, I am the prime cause in all respects of gods as well as of the great seers. (2)

यो मामजमनादिं च वेत्ति लोकमहेश्वरम्।
असम्मूढः स मर्त्येषु सर्वपापैः प्रमुच्यते॥ ३॥

He who knows Me in reality as birthless and without beginning, and as the supreme Lord of the Universe, he, undeluded among men, is purged of all sins. (3)

बुद्धिर्ज्ञानमसम्मोहः क्षमा सत्यं दमः शमः।
सुखं दुःखं भवोऽभावो भयं चाभयमेव च॥ ४॥

अहिंसा समता तुष्टिस्तपो दानं यशोऽयशः।
भवन्ति भावा भूतानां मत्त एव पृथग्विधाः॥ ५॥

Reason, right knowledge, unclouded understanding, forbearance, veracity, control over the senses and mind, joy and sorrow, evolution and dissolution, fear and fearlessness, non-violence, equanimity, contentment, austerity, charity, fame and obloquy—these diverse traits of creatures emanate from Me alone. (4-5)

महर्षयः सप्त पूर्वे चत्वारो मनवस्तथा।
मद्भावा मानसा जाता येषां लोक इमाः प्रजाः॥ ६॥

The seven great seers, their four elders (Sanaka and others), and the fourteen Manus or progenitors of mankind (such as Svāyambhuva and his successors), who were all devoted to Me, were born of My will; from them all these creatures in the world have descended. (6)

एतां विभूतिं योगं च मम यो वेत्ति तत्त्वतः।
सोऽविकम्पेन योगेन युज्यते नात्र संशयः॥ ७॥

He who knows in reality this supreme divine glory and supernatural power of Mine, gets established in Me through unfaltering devotion; of this there is no doubt. (7)

अहं सर्वस्य प्रभवो मत्तः सर्वं प्रवर्तते।
इति मत्वा भजन्ते मां बुधा भावसमन्विताः॥ ८॥

I am the source of all creation and everything in the world moves because of Me; knowing thus, the wise, full of devotion, constantly worship Me. (8)

मच्चित्ता मद्गतप्राणा बोधयन्तः परस्परम्।
कथयन्तश्च मां नित्यं तुष्यन्ति च रमन्ति च॥ ९ ॥

With their minds fixed on Me, and their lives surrendered to Me, conversing and enlightening one another about My glories, My devotees ever remain contented and take delight in Me. (9)

तेषां सततयुक्तानां भजतां प्रीतिपूर्वकम्।
ददामि बुद्धियोगं तं येन मामुपयान्ति ते॥ १० ॥

On those ever united through meditation with Me and worshipping Me with love, I confer that Yoga of wisdom by which they come to Me. (10)

तेषामेवानुकम्पार्थमहमज्ञानजं तमः।
नाशयाम्यात्मभावस्थो ज्ञानदीपेन भास्वता॥ ११ ॥

In order to bestow My compassion on them, I, dwelling in their hearts, dispel their darkness born of ignorance by the illuminating lamp of knowledge. (11)

अर्जुन उवाच

परं ब्रह्म परं धाम पवित्रं परमं भवान्।
पुरुषं शाश्वतं दिव्यमादिदेवमजं विभुम्॥ १२ ॥
आहुस्त्वामृषयः सर्वे देवर्षिर्नारदस्तथा।
असितो देवलो व्यासः स्वयं चैव ब्रवीषि मे॥ १३ ॥

Arjuna said : You are the transcendent Eternal, the supreme Abode and the greatest purifier; all the seers speak of You as the eternal divine Puruṣa, the primal Deity, unborn and all-pervading.

Likewise speak the celestial sage Nārada, the sages Asita and Devala and the great sage Vyāsa; and Yourself too proclaim this to me. (12-13)

सर्वमेतदृतं मन्ये यन्मां वदसि केशव।
न हि ते भगवन्व्यक्तिं विदुर्देवा न दानवाः॥ १४॥

Kṛṣṇa, I believe as true all that You tell me. Lord, neither demons nor gods are aware of Your manifestations. (14)

स्वयमेवात्मनात्मानं वेत्थ त्वं पुरुषोत्तम।
भूतभावन भूतेश देवदेव जगत्पते॥ १५॥

O Creator of beings, O Ruler of creatures, god of gods, the Lord of the universe, O supreme Puruṣa, You alone know what You are by Yourself. (15)

वक्तुमर्हस्यशेषेण दिव्या ह्यात्मविभूतयः।
याभिर्विभूतिभिर्लोकानिमांस्त्वं व्याप्य तिष्ठसि॥ १६॥

Therefore, You alone can describe in full Your divine glories, whereby You pervade all these worlds. (16)

कथं विद्यामहं योगिंस्त्वां सदा परिचिन्तयन्।
केषु केषु च भावेषु चिन्त्योऽसि भगवन्मया॥ १७॥

O Master of Yoga, through what process of continuous meditation shall I know You? And in what particular forms, O Lord, are You to be meditated upon by me? (17)

विस्तरेणात्मनो योगं विभूतिं च जनार्दन।
भूयः कथय तृप्तिर्हि शृण्वतो नास्ति मेऽमृतम्॥ १८॥

Kṛṣṇa, tell me once more in detail Your power of Yoga and Your glory; for I know no satiety in hearing Your nectar-like words. (18)

श्रीभगवानुवाच

हन्त ते कथयिष्यामि दिव्या ह्यात्मविभूतयः।
प्राधान्यतः कुरुश्रेष्ठ नास्त्यन्तो विस्तरस्य मे॥ १९॥

Śrī Bhagavān said : Arjuna, now I shall tell you My prominent divine glories; for there is no limit to My manifestations. (19)

अहमात्मा गुडाकेश सर्वभूताशयस्थितः।
अहमादिश्च मध्यं च भूतानामन्त एव च॥ २०॥

Arjuna, I am the universal Self seated in the hearts of all beings; so, I alone am the beginning, the middle and also the end of all beings. (20)

आदित्यानामहं विष्णुर्ज्योतिषां रविरंशुमान्।
मरीचिर्मरुतामस्मि नक्षत्राणामहं शशी॥ २१॥

I am Viṣṇu among the twelve sons of Aditi, and the radiant sun among the luminaries; I am the glow of the Maruts (the forty-nine wind-gods), and the moon, the lord of the stars. (21)

वेदानां सामवेदोऽस्मि देवानामस्मि वासवः।
इन्द्रियाणां मनश्चास्मि भूतानामस्मि चेतना॥ २२॥

Among the Vedas, I am the Sāmaveda; among the gods, I am Indra. Among the organs of perception i.e., senses, I am the mind; and I am the consciousness (life-energy) in living beings. (22)

रुद्राणां शङ्करश्चास्मि वित्तेशो यक्षरक्षसाम्।
वसूनां पावकश्चास्मि मेरुः शिखरिणामहम्॥ २३॥

Among the eleven Rudras (gods of destruction), I am Śiva; and among the Yakṣas and Rākṣasas, I am the lord of riches (Kubera). Among the eight Vasus, I am the god of fire; and among the mountains, I am the Meru. (23)

पुरोधसां च मुख्यं मां विद्धि पार्थ बृहस्पतिम्।
सेनानीनामहं स्कन्दः सरसामस्मि सागरः॥ २४॥

Among the priests, Arjuna, know Me to be their chief, Bṛhaspati. Among warrior-chiefs, I am Skanda (the generalissimo of the gods); and among the reservoirs of water, I am the ocean. (24)

महर्षीणां भृगुरहं गिरामस्म्येकमक्षरम्।
यज्ञानां जपयज्ञोऽस्मि स्थावराणां हिमालयः॥ २५॥

Among the great seers, I am Bhṛgu; among words, I am the sacred syllable OM; among sacrifices, I am the sacrifice of Japa (muttering of sacred formulas); and among the immovables, the Himālayas. (25)

अश्वत्थः सर्ववृक्षाणां देवर्षीणां च नारदः।
गन्धर्वाणां चित्ररथः सिद्धानां कपिलो मुनिः॥ २६॥

Among all trees, I am Aśvattha (the holy fig tree); among the celestial sages, Nārada; among the Gandharvas (celestial musicians), Citraratha, and among the Siddhas, I am the sage Kapila. (26)

उच्चैःश्रवसमश्वानां विद्धि माममृतोद्भवम्।
ऐरावतं गजेन्द्राणां नराणां च नराधिपम्॥ २७॥

Among horses, know me to be the celestial horse Uccaiḥśravā, begotten of the churning of the ocean along with nectar; among mighty elephants, Airāvata (Indra's elephant); and among men, the king.(27)

आयुधानामहं वज्रं धेनूनामस्मि कामधुक्।
प्रजनश्चास्मि कन्दर्पः सर्पाणामस्मि वासुकिः॥ २८॥

Among weapons, I am the thunderbolt; among cows, I am the celestial cow Kāmadhenu (the cow of plenty). I am the sexual desire which leads to procreation (as enjoined by the scriptures); among serpents, I am Vāsuki. (28)

अनन्तश्चास्मि नागानां वरुणो यादसामहम्।
पितॄणामर्यमा चास्मि यमः संयमतामहम्॥ २९॥

Among Nāgas (a special class of serpents), I am the serpent-god Ananta; and I am Varuṇa, the lord of aquatic creatures. Among the manes, I am Aryamā (the head of the Pitṛs); and among rulers, I am Yama (the god of death). (29)

प्रह्लादश्चास्मि दैत्यानां कालः कलयतामहम्।
मृगाणां च मृगेन्द्रोऽहं वैनतेयश्च पक्षिणाम्॥ ३०॥

Among the Daityas, I am the great devotee Prahlāda; and of calculators, I am Time; among quadrupeds, I am the lion; and among birds, I am Garuḍa. (30)

पवनः पवतामस्मि रामः शस्त्रभृतामहम्।
झषाणां मकरश्चास्मि स्रोतसामस्मि जाह्नवी॥ ३१॥

Among purifiers, I am the wind; among wielders of arms, I am Śrī Rāma. Among fishes, I am the shark; and among streams, I am the Ganges. (31)

सर्गाणामादिरन्तश्च मध्यं चैवाहमर्जुन।
अध्यात्मविद्या विद्यानां वादः प्रवदतामहम्॥ ३२॥

Arjuna, I am the beginning, the middle and the end of all creations. Of all knowledge, I am the knowledge of the soul (metaphysics); among disputants, I am the right type of discussion. (32)

अक्षराणामकारोऽस्मि द्वन्द्वः सामासिकस्य च।
अहमेवाक्षयः कालो धाताहं विश्वतोमुखः॥ ३३॥

Among the sounds represented by the various letters, I am 'A' (the sound represented by the first letter of the alphabet); of the different kinds of compounds in grammar, I am the copulative compound. I am verily the endless Time (the devourer of Time, God); I am the sustainer of all, having My face on all sides. (33)

मृत्युः सर्वहरश्चाहमुद्भवश्च भविष्यताम्।
कीर्तिः श्रीर्वाक्च नारीणां स्मृतिर्मेधा धृतिः क्षमा॥ ३४॥

I am the all-destroying Death that annihilates all, and the origin of all that are to be born. Of feminities, I am Kīrti, Śrī,Vāk, Smṛti, Medhā, Dhṛti and Kṣamā (the goddesses presiding over glory, prosperity, speech, memory, intelligence, fortitude and forbearance, respectively). (34)

बृहत्साम तथा साम्नां गायत्री छन्दसामहम्।
मासानां मार्गशीर्षोऽहमृतूनां कुसुमाकरः॥ ३५॥

Likewise, among the Śrutis that can be sung, I am the variety known as Bṛhatsāma; while among the Vedic hymns, I am the hymn known as Gāyatrī. Again, among the twelve months of the Hindu calendar, I am the month known as 'Mārgaśīrṣa' (corresponding approximately to November-December); and among the six seasons (successively appearing in India in the course of a year), I am the spring season.(35)

द्यूतं छलयतामस्मि तेजस्तेजस्विनामहम्।
जयोऽस्मि व्यवसायोऽस्मि सत्त्वं सत्त्ववतामहम्॥ ३६॥

I am gambling among deceitful practices, and the glory of the glorious. I am the victory of the victorious, the resolve of the resolute, the goodness of the good. (36)

वृष्णीनां वासुदेवोऽस्मि पाण्डवानां धनञ्जयः।
मुनीनामप्यहं व्यासः कवीनामुशना कविः॥ ३७॥

I am Kṛṣṇa among the Vṛṣṇis, Arjuna among the sons of Pāṇḍu, Vyāsa among the sages, and the sage Śukrācārya among the wise. (37)

दण्डो दमयतामस्मि नीतिरस्मि जिगीषताम्।
मौनं चैवास्मि गुह्यानां ज्ञानं ज्ञानवतामहम्॥ ३८॥

I am the subduing power of rulers; I am righteousness in those who seek to conquer. Of things to be kept secret, I am the custodian in the form of reticence; and I am the wisdom of the wise. (38)

यच्चापि सर्वभूतानां बीजं तदहमर्जुन।
न तदस्ति विना यत्स्यान्मया भूतं चराचरम्॥ ३९॥

Arjuna, I am even that, which is the seed of all life. For there is no creature, moving or unmoving, which can exist without Me. (39)

नान्तोऽस्ति मम दिव्यानां विभूतीनां परन्तप।
एष तूद्देशतः प्रोक्तो विभूतेर्विस्तरो मया॥ ४०॥

Arjuna, there is no limit to My divine manifestations. This is only a brief description by Me of the extent of My glory. (40)

यद्यद्विभूतिमत्सत्त्वं श्रीमदूर्जितमेव वा।
तत्तदेवावगच्छ त्वं मम तेजोंऽशसम्भवम्॥ ४१॥

Every such being as is glorious, brilliant and powerful, know that to be a part manifestation of My glory. (41)

अथवा बहुनैतेन किं ज्ञातेन तवार्जुन।
विष्टभ्याहमिदं कृत्स्नमेकांशेन स्थितो जगत्॥ ४२॥

Or, what will you gain by knowing all this in detail, Arjuna? Suffice it to say that I hold this entire universe by a fraction of My Yogic Power. (42)

ॐ तत्सदिति श्रीमद्भगवद्गीतासूपनिषत्सु ब्रह्मविद्यायां
योगशास्त्रे श्रीकृष्णार्जुनसंवादे विभूतियोगो
नाम दशमोऽध्यायः॥ १०॥

Thus, in the Upaniṣad sung by the Lord, the Science of Brahma, the scripture of Yoga, the dialogue between Śrī Kṛṣṇa and Arjuna, ends the tenth chapter entitled "The Yoga of Divine Glories."

Chapter XI

अर्जुन उवाच

मदनुग्रहाय परमं गुह्यमध्यात्मसञ्ज्ञितम्।
यत्त्वयोक्तं वचस्तेन मोहोऽयं विगतो मम॥ १॥

Arjuna said : Thanks to the most profound words of spiritual wisdom that You have spoken out of kindness to me, this delusion of mine has entirely disappeared. (1)

भवाप्ययौ हि भूतानां श्रुतौ विस्तरशो मया।
त्वत्तः कमलपत्राक्ष माहात्म्यमपि चाव्ययम्॥ २॥

For, Kṛṣṇa, I have heard from You in detail an account of the evolution and dissolution of beings, and also Your immortal glory. (2)

एवमेतद्यथात्थ त्वमात्मानं परमेश्वर।
द्रष्टुमिच्छामि ते रूपमैश्वरं पुरुषोत्तम॥ ३॥

Lord, You are precisely what You declare Yourself to be. But I long to see Your divine form possessed of wisdom, glory, energy, strength, valour and effulgence, O Puruṣottama, the Supreme Being! (3)

मन्यसे यदि तच्छक्यं मया द्रष्टुमिति प्रभो।
योगेश्वर ततो मे त्वं दर्शयात्मानमव्ययम्॥ ४॥

Kṛṣṇa, if You think that it can be seen by me,

then, O Lord of Yoga, reveal to me Your imperishable form. (4)

श्रीभगवानुवाच

पश्य मे पार्थ रूपाणि शतशोऽथ सहस्रशः।
नानाविधानि दिव्यानि नानावर्णाकृतीनि च॥ ५॥

Śrī Bhagavān said: Arjuna, behold My manifold, multifarious divine forms of various colours and shapes, in their hundreds and thousands. (5)

पश्यादित्यान्वसून्रुद्रानश्विनौ मरुतस्तथा।
बहून्यदृष्टपूर्वाणि पश्याश्चर्याणि भारत॥ ६॥

Behold in Me, Arjuna, the twelve sons of Aditi, the eight Vasus, the eleven Rudras (gods of destruction), the two Aśvinīkumāras (the twin-born physicians of gods) and the forty-nine Maruts (wind-gods), and witness many more wonderful forms never seen before. (6)

इहैकस्थं जगत्कृत्स्नं पश्याद्य सचराचरम्।
मम देहे गुडाकेश यच्चान्यद्द्रष्टुमिच्छसि॥ ७॥

Arjuna, behold as concentrated within this body of Mine the entire creation consisting of both the moving and the unmoving beings, and whatever else you desire to see. (7)

न तु मां शक्यसे द्रष्टुमनेनैव स्वचक्षुषा।
दिव्यं ददामि ते चक्षुः पश्य मे योगमैश्वरम्॥ ८॥

But surely you cannot see Me with these physical eyes of yours; therefore, I vouchsafe to you the divine eye. With this you behold My divine power of Yoga. (8)

सञ्जय उवाच

एवमुक्त्वा ततो राजन्महायोगेश्वरो हरिः।
दर्शयामास पार्थाय परमं रूपमैश्वरम्॥ ९ ॥

Sañjaya said : My lord! having spoken thus, Śrī Kṛṣṇa, the supreme Master of Yoga, forthwith revealed to Arjuna His supremely glorious divine Form. (9)

अनेकवक्त्रनयनमनेकाद्भुतदर्शनम्।
अनेकदिव्याभरणं दिव्यानेकोद्यतायुधम्॥ १० ॥
दिव्यमाल्याम्बरधरं दिव्यगन्धानुलेपनम्।
सर्वाश्चर्यमयं देवमनन्तं विश्वतोमुखम्॥ ११ ॥

Arjuna saw the supreme Deity possessing many mouths and eyes, presenting many a wonderful sight, decked with many divine ornaments, wielding many uplifted divine weapons, wearing divine garlands and vestments, anointed all over with divine fragrances, full of all wonders, infinite and having faces on all sides. (10-11)

दिवि सूर्यसहस्रस्य भवेद्युगपदुत्थिता।
यदि भाः सदृशी सा स्याद्भासस्तस्य महात्मनः॥ १२ ॥

If there be the effulgence of a thousand suns bursting forth all at once in the heavens, even that would hardly approach the splendour of the mighty Lord. (12)

तत्रैकस्थं जगत्कृत्स्नं प्रविभक्तमनेकधा।
अपश्यद्देवदेवस्य शरीरे पाण्डवस्तदा॥ १३॥

Concentrated at one place in the person of that supreme Deity, Arjuna then beheld the whole universe with its manifold divisions. (13)

ततः स विस्मयाविष्टो हृष्टरोमा धनञ्जयः।
प्रणम्य शिरसा देवं कृताञ्जलिरभाषत॥ १४॥

Then Arjuna, full of wonder and with the hair standing on end, reverentially bowed his head to the divine Lord, and with folded hands addressed Him thus. (14)

अर्जुन उवाच

पश्यामि देवांस्तव देव देहे
सर्वांस्तथा भूतविशेषसङ्घान्।
ब्रह्माणमीशं कमलासनस्थ-
मृषींश्च सर्वानुरगांश्च दिव्यान्॥ १५॥

Arjuna said : Lord, I behold within Your body all gods and hosts of different beings, Brahmā throned on his lotus-seat, Śiva and all Ṛṣis and celestial serpents. (15)

अनेकबाहूदरवक्त्रनेत्रं-
पश्यामि त्वां सर्वतोऽनन्तरूपम्।
नान्तं न मध्यं न पुनस्तवादिं-
पश्यामि विश्वेश्वर विश्वरूप॥ १६॥

O Lord of the universe, I see You endowed with numerous arms, bellies, mouths, and eyes and having innumerable forms extended on all sides. O Lord, manifested in the form of the universe, I see neither Your beginning nor middle, nor even Your end. (16)

किरीटिनं गदिनं चक्रिणं च
तेजोराशिं सर्वतो दीप्तिमन्तम्।
पश्यामि त्वां दुर्निरीक्ष्यं समन्ता-
द्दीप्तानलार्कद्युतिमप्रमेयम् ॥ १७॥

I see you endowed with diadem, club and discus, a mass of splendour glowing all round, having the brilliance of a blazing fire and the sun, hard to gaze at and immeasurable on all sides. (17)

त्वमक्षरं परमं वेदितव्यं-
त्वमस्य विश्वस्य परं निधानम्।
त्वमव्ययः शाश्वतधर्मगोप्ता
सनातनस्त्वं पुरुषो मतो मे ॥ १८॥

You are the supreme indestructible worthy of being known; you are the ultimate refuge of this universe. You are, again, the protector of the ageless Dharma; I consider You to be the eternal imperishable Being. (18)

अनादिमध्यान्तमनन्तवीर्य-
मनन्तबाहुं शशिसूर्यनेत्रम्।
पश्यामि त्वां दीप्तहुताशवक्त्रं-
स्वतेजसा विश्वमिदं तपन्तम् ॥ १९॥

I see You without beginning, middle or end, possessing unlimited prowess and endowed with numberless arms, having the moon and the sun for Your eyes, and blazing fire for Your mouth, and scorching this universe by Your radiance. (19)

द्यावापृथिव्योरिदमन्तरं हि
व्याप्तं त्वयैकेन दिशश्च सर्वाः।
दृष्ट्वाद्भुतं रूपमुग्रं तवेदं
लोकत्रयं प्रव्यथितं महात्मन्॥ २०॥

Yonder space between heaven and earth and all the quarters are entirely filled by You alone. Seeing this transcendent, dreadful Form of Yours, O Soul of the universe, all the three worlds feel greatly perturbed. (20)

अमी हि त्वां सुरसङ्घा विशन्ति
केचिद्भीताः प्राञ्जलयो गृणन्ति।
स्वस्तीत्युक्त्वा महर्षिसिद्धसङ्घाः
स्तुवन्ति त्वां स्तुतिभिः पुष्कलाभिः॥ २१॥

Yonder hosts of gods are entering You; some with palms joined out of fear are recounting Your names and glories. Multitudes of Maharṣis and Siddhas, saying 'Let there be peace', are extolling You by means of excellent hymns. (21)

रुद्रादित्या वसवो ये च साध्या
विश्वेऽश्विनौ मरुतश्चोष्मपाश्च।

गन्धर्वयक्षासुरसिद्धसङ्घा-
वीक्षन्ते त्वां विस्मिताश्चैव सर्वे॥ २२॥

The eleven Rudras, twelve Ādityas and eight Vasus, the Sādhyas and Viśvedevas, the two Aśvinīkumāras and forty-nine Maruts, as well as the manes and multitudes of Gandharvas, Yakṣas, Asuras and Siddhas, all these gaze upon You in amazement. (22)

रूपं महत्ते बहुवक्त्रनेत्रं-
महाबाहो बहुबाहूरुपादम्।
बहूदरं बहुदंष्ट्राकरालं-
दृष्ट्वा लोकाः प्रव्यथितास्तथाहम्॥ २३॥

Lord, seeing this stupendous and dreadful Form of Yours, possessing numerous mouths and eyes, many arms, thighs and feet, many bellies and many teeth, the worlds are terror-struck; so am I. (23)

नभःस्पृशं दीप्तमनेकवर्णं-
व्यात्ताननं दीप्तविशालनेत्रम्।
दृष्ट्वा हि त्वां प्रव्यथितान्तरात्मा
धृतिं न विन्दामि शमं च विष्णो॥ २४॥

Lord, seeing Your Form reaching the heavens, effulgent multi-coloured, having its mouth wide open and possessing large flaming eyes, I, with my inmost self frightened, have lost self-control and find no peace. (24)

दंष्ट्राकरालानि च ते मुखानि
दृष्ट्वैव कालानलसन्निभानि।

दिशो न जाने न लभे च शर्म
प्रसीद देवेश जगन्निवास॥ २५॥

Seeing Your faces frightful on account of teeth therein and blazing like the fire at the time of universal destruction, I am utterly bewildered and find no happiness; therefore, have mercy on me, O Lord of celestials! O Abode of the universe! (25)

अमी च त्वां धृतराष्ट्रस्य पुत्राः
सर्वे सहैवावनिपालसङ्घैः।
भीष्मो द्रोणः सूतपुत्रस्तथासौ
सहास्मदीयैरपि योधमुख्यैः॥ २६॥
वक्त्राणि ते त्वरमाणा विशन्ति
दंष्ट्राकरालानि भयानकानि।
केचिद्विलग्ना दशनान्तरेषु
सन्दृश्यन्ते चूर्णितैरुत्तमाङ्गैः॥ २७॥

All those sons of Dhṛtarāṣṭra with hosts of kings are entering You. Bhīṣma, Droṇa and yonder Karṇa, with the principal warriors on our side as well, are rushing headlong into Your fearful mouths looking all the more terrible on account of the teeth; some are seen stuck up in the gaps between Your teeth with their heads crushed. (26-27)

यथा नदीनां बहवोऽम्बुवेगाः
समुद्रमेवाभिमुखा द्रवन्ति।
तथा तवामी नरलोकवीरा-
विशन्ति वक्त्राण्यभिविज्वलन्ति॥ २८॥

As the myriad streams of rivers rush towards the sea alone, so do those warriors of the mortal world enter Your flaming mouths. (28)

यथा प्रदीप्तं ज्वलनं पतङ्गा-
विशन्ति नाशाय समृद्धवेगाः।
तथैव नाशाय विशन्ति लोका-
स्तवापि वक्त्राणि समृद्धवेगाः॥ २९॥

As moths rush with great speed into the blazing fire for extinction out of 'Moha', even so, all these people are with great rapidity entering Your mouths to meet their doom. (29)

लेलिह्यसे ग्रसमानः समन्ता-
ल्लोकान्समग्रान्वदनैर्ज्वलद्भिः।
तेजोभिरापूर्य जगत्समग्रं-
भासस्तवोग्राः प्रतपन्ति विष्णो॥ ३०॥

Devouring all the worlds through Your flaming mouths and licking them on all sides, O Lord Viṣṇu! Your fiery rays fill the whole universe with their fierce radiance and are scorching it. (30)

आख्याहि मे को भवानुग्ररूपो-
नमोऽस्तु ते देववर प्रसीद।
विज्ञातुमिच्छामि भवन्तमाद्यं-
न हि प्रजानामि तव प्रवृत्तिम्॥ ३१॥

Tell me who You are with a form so terrible? My obeisance to You, O best of gods; be kind to me. I wish to know You, the Primal Being, in particular; for I know not what you intend to do. (31)

श्रीभगवानुवाच

कालोऽस्मि लोकक्षयकृत्प्रवृद्धो-
लोकान्समाहर्तुमिह प्रवृत्तः।
ऋतेऽपि त्वां न भविष्यन्ति सर्वे
येऽवस्थिताः प्रत्यनीकेषु योधाः॥ ३२॥

Śrī Bhagavān said: I am mighty Kāla (the eternal Time-spirit), the destroyer of the worlds. I am out to exterminate these people. Even without you all those warriors, arrayed in the enemy's camp, shall die. (32)

तस्मात्त्वमुत्तिष्ठ यशो लभस्व
जित्वा शत्रून्भुङ्क्ष्व राज्यं समृद्धम्।
मयैवैते निहताः पूर्वमेव
निमित्तमात्रं भव सव्यसाचिन्॥ ३३॥

Therefore, do you arise and win glory; conquering foes, enjoy the affluent kingdom. These warriors stand already slain by Me; be you only an instrument, Arjuna. (33)

द्रोणं च भीष्मं च जयद्रथं च
कर्णं तथान्यानपि योधवीरान्।
मया हतांस्त्वं जहि मा व्यथिष्ठा-
युध्यस्व जेतासि रणे सपत्नान्॥ ३४॥

Do kill Droṇa and Bhīṣma and Jayadratha and Karṇa and other brave warriors, who already stand killed by Me; fear not. Fight and you will surely conquer the enemies in the war. (34)

सञ्जय उवाच

एतच्छुत्वा वचनं केशवस्य
कृताञ्जलिर्वेपमानः किरीटी।
नमस्कृत्वा भूय एवाह कृष्णं-
सगद्गदं भीतभीतः प्रणम्य॥ ३५॥

Sañjaya said : Hearing these words of Bhagavān Keśava, Arjuna tremblingly bowed to Him with joined palms, and bowing again in extreme terror spoke to Śrī Kṛṣṇa in faltering accents. (35)

अर्जुन उवाच

स्थाने हृषीकेश तव प्रकीर्त्या
जगत्प्रहृष्यत्यनुरज्यते च।
रक्षांसि भीतानि दिशो द्रवन्ति
सर्वे नमस्यन्ति च सिद्धसङ्घाः॥ ३६॥

Arjuna said : Lord, well it is, the universe exults and is filled with love by chanting Your names, virtues and glory; terrified Rākṣasas are fleeing in all directions, and all the hosts of Siddhas are bowing to You. (36)

कस्माच्च ते न नमेरन्महात्मन्
गरीयसे ब्रह्मणोऽप्यादिकर्त्रे।
अनन्त देवेश जगन्निवास
त्वमक्षरं सदसत्तत्परं यत्॥ ३७॥

O Great soul, why should they not bow to you, who are the progenitor of Brahmā himself and the greatest of the great? O infinite, O Lord of celestials, O Abode of the universe, You are that which is existent (Sat), that which is non-existent (Asat) and also that which is beyond both, viz., the indestructible Brahma. (37)

त्वमादिदेवः पुरुषः पुराण-
स्त्वमस्य विश्वस्य परं निधानम्।
वेत्तासि वेद्यं च परं च धाम
त्वया ततं विश्वमनन्तरूप ॥ ३८ ॥

You are the primal Deity, the most ancient Person; You are the ultimate resort of this universe. You are both the knower and the knowable, and the highest abode. It is You who pervade the universe, O one assuming endless forms. (38)

वायुर्यमोऽग्निर्वरुणः शशाङ्कः
प्रजापतिस्त्वं प्रपितामहश्च।
नमो नमस्तेऽस्तु सहस्रकृत्वः
पुनश्च भूयोऽपि नमो नमस्ते ॥ ३९ ॥

You are Vāyu (the wind-god), Yama (the god of death), Agni (the god of fire), Varuṇa (the god of water), the moon-god, Brahmā (the Lord of creation), nay, the father of Brahmā himself. Hail, hail to You a thousand times; salutations, repeated salutations to You once again. (39)

नमः पुरस्तादथ पृष्ठतस्ते
नमोऽस्तु ते सर्वत एव सर्व।
अनन्तवीर्यामितविक्रमस्त्वं-
सर्वं समाप्नोषि ततोऽसि सर्वः ॥ ४० ॥

O Lord of infinite prowess, my salutations to

You from the front and from behind. O soul of all, my obeisance to You from all sides indeed. You, who possess infinite might, pervade all; therefore, You are all. (40)

सखेति मत्वा प्रसभं यदुक्तं-
हे कृष्ण हे यादव हे सखेति।
अजानता महिमानं तवेदं-
मया प्रमादात्प्रणयेन वापि॥ ४१॥
यच्चावहासार्थमसत्कृतोऽसि
विहारशय्यासनभोजनेषु ।
एकोऽथवाप्यच्युत तत्समक्षं-
तत्क्षामये त्वामहमप्रमेयम्॥ ४२॥

The way in which I have importunately called You, either through intimacy or thoughtlessly, "Ho Kṛṣṇa! Ho Yādava! Ho Comrade!" and so on, unaware of the greatness of Yours, and thinking You only to be a friend, and the way in which O Acyuta! the Infallible! You have been slighted by me in jest, while at play, reposing, sitting or at meals, either alone or even in the presence of others—for all that, O Immeasurable Lord, I crave forgiveness from You. (41-42)

पितासि लोकस्य चराचरस्य
त्वमस्य पूज्यश्च गुरुर्गरीयान्।
न त्वत्समोऽस्त्यभ्यधिकः कुतोऽन्यो-
लोकत्रयेऽप्यप्रतिमप्रभाव ॥ ४३॥

You are the Father of this moving and unmoving creation, nay, the greatest teacher worthy of adoration. O Lord of incomparable might, in all the three worlds there is none else even equal to You; how, then, can anyone be greater than You? (43)

तस्मात्प्रणम्य प्रणिधाय कायं-
प्रसादये त्वामहमीशमीड्यम्।
पितेव पुत्रस्य सखेव सख्युः
प्रियः प्रियायार्हसि देव सोढुम्॥ ४४॥

Therefore, Lord, prostrating my body at Your feet and bowing low I seek to propitiate You, the ruler of all and worthy of all praise. It behoves You to bear with me even as a father bears with his son, a friend with his friend and a husband with his beloved spouse. (44)

अदृष्टपूर्वं हृषितोऽस्मि दृष्ट्वा
भयेन च प्रव्यथितं मनो मे।
तदेव मे दर्शय देवरूपं-
प्रसीद देवेश जगन्निवास॥ ४५॥

Having seen Your wondrous form, which was never seen before, I feel transported with joy; at the same time my mind is tormented by fear. Pray! reveal to me that divine form, the form of Viṣṇu with four-arms; O Lord of celestials, O Abode of the universe, be gracious. (45)

किरीटिनं गदिनं चक्रहस्त-
मिच्छामि त्वां द्रष्टुमहं तथैव।
तेनैव रूपेण चतुर्भुजेन
सहस्रबाहो भव विश्वमूर्ते॥ ४६॥

I wish to see You adorned in the same way

with a diadem on the head, and holding a mace and a discus in two of Your hands. O Lord with a thousand arms, O Universal Being, appear again in the same four-armed Form. (46)

श्रीभगवानुवाच

मया प्रसन्नेन तवार्जुनेदं-
रूपं परं दर्शितमात्मयोगात्।
तेजोमयं विश्वमनन्तमाद्यं-
यन्मे त्वदन्येन न दृष्टपूर्वम्॥ ४७॥

Śrī Bhagavān said : Arjuna! pleased with you I have shown you, through My power of Yoga, this supreme, effulgent, primal and infinite Cosmic Form, which has never been seen before by anyone other than you. (47)

न वेदयज्ञाध्ययनैर्न दानै-
र्न च क्रियाभिर्न तपोभिरुग्रैः।
एवंरूपः शक्य अहं नृलोके
द्रष्टुं त्वदन्येन कुरुप्रवीर॥ ४८॥

Arjuna, in this mortal world I cannot be seen in this Form by anyone other than you, either through the study of the Vedas or by rituals, or, again, through gifts, actions or austere penances.(48)

मा ते व्यथा मा च विमूढभावो-
दृष्ट्वा रूपं घोरमीदृङ्ममेदम्।
व्यपेतभीः प्रीतमनाः पुनस्त्वं-
तदेव मे रूपमिदं प्रपश्य॥ ४९॥

Seeing such a dreadful Form of Mine as this,

do not be perturbed or perplexed; with a fearless and tranquil mind, behold once again the same four-armed Form of Mine bearing the conch, discus, mace and lotus. (49)

सञ्जय उवाच

इत्यर्जुनं वासुदेवस्तथोक्त्वा
स्वकं रूपं दर्शयामास भूयः।
आश्वासयामास च भीतमेनं-
भूत्वा पुनः सौम्यवपुर्महात्मा॥ ५०॥

Sañjaya said : Having spoken thus to Arjuna, Bhagavān Vāsudeva again revealed to him His own four-armed Form; and then, assuming a genial form, the high-souled Śrī Kṛṣṇa consoled the frightened Arjuna. (50)

अर्जुन उवाच

दृष्ट्वेदं मानुषं रूपं तव सौम्यं जनार्दन।
इदानीमस्मि संवृत्तः सचेताः प्रकृतिं गतः॥ ५१॥

Arjuna said : Kṛṣṇa, seeing this gentle human form of Yours I have regained my composure and am my ownself again. (51)

श्रीभगवानुवाच

सुदुर्दर्शमिदं रूपं दृष्टवानसि यन्मम।
देवा अप्यस्य रूपस्य नित्यं दर्शनकाङ्क्षिणः॥ ५२॥

Śrī Bhagavān said : This form of Mine (with four-arms) which you have just seen, is exceedingly difficult to behold. Even the gods are always eager to see this form. (52)

नाहं वेदैर्न तपसा न दानेन न चेज्यया।
शक्य एवंविधो द्रष्टुं दृष्टवानसि मां यथा॥ ५३॥

Neither by study of the Vedas, nor by penance, nor again by charity, nor even by rituals can I be seen in this form (with four-arms) as you have seen Me. (53)

भक्त्या त्वनन्यया शक्य अहमेवंविधोऽर्जुन।
ज्ञातुं द्रष्टुं च तत्त्वेन प्रवेष्टुं च परन्तप॥ ५४॥

Through single-minded devotion, however, I can be seen in this form (with four-arms), nay, known in essence and even entered into, O valiant Arjuna. (54)

मत्कर्मकृन्मत्परमो मद्भक्तः सङ्गवर्जितः।
निर्वैरः सर्वभूतेषु यः स मामेति पाण्डव॥ ५५॥

Arjuna, he who performs all his duties for My sake, depends on Me, is devoted to Me, has no attachment, and is free from malice towards all beings, reaches Me. (55)

ॐ तत्सदिति श्रीमद्भगवद्गीतासूपनिषत्सु ब्रह्मविद्यायां
योगशास्त्रे श्रीकृष्णार्जुनसंवादे विश्वरूपदर्शनयोगो
नामैकादशोऽध्यायः॥ ११॥

Thus, in the Upaniṣad sung by the Lord, the Science of Brahma, the scripture of Yoga, the dialogue between Śrī Kṛṣṇa and Arjuna, ends the eleventh chapter entitled "The Yoga of the Vision of the Universal Form."

Chapter XII

अर्जुन उवाच

एवं सततयुक्ता ये भक्तास्त्वां पर्युपासते।
ये चाप्यक्षरमव्यक्तं तेषां के योगवित्तमाः ॥ १ ॥

Arjuna said : The devotees exclusively and constantly devoted to You in the manner stated just earlier, adore You as possessed of form and attributes, and those who adore as the supreme Reality only the indestructible unmanifest Brahma (who is Truth, Knowledge and Bliss solidified)—of these two types of worshippers who are the best knowers of Yoga? (1)

श्रीभगवानुवाच

मय्यावेश्य मनो ये मां नित्ययुक्ता उपासते।
श्रद्धया परयोपेतास्ते मे युक्ततमा मताः ॥ २ ॥

Śrī Bhagavān said : I consider them to be the best Yogīs, who endowed with supreme faith, and ever united through meditation with Me, worship Me with their mind centred on Me. (2)

ये त्वक्षरमनिर्देश्यमव्यक्तं पर्युपासते।
सर्वत्रगमचिन्त्यं च कूटस्थमचलं ध्रुवम् ॥ ३ ॥
सन्नियम्येन्द्रियग्रामं सर्वत्र समबुद्धयः।
ते प्राप्नुवन्ति मामेव सर्वभूतहिते रताः ॥ ४ ॥

Those, however, who fully controlling all their senses and even-minded towards all, and devoted to the welfare of all beings, constantly adore as their very self the unthinkable, omnipresent, indestructible, indefinable, eternal, immovable, unmanifest and changeless Brahma, they too come to Me. (3-4)

क्लेशोऽधिकतरस्तेषामव्यक्तासक्तचेतसाम् ।
अव्यक्ता हि गतिर्दुःखं देहवद्भिरवाप्यते ॥ ५ ॥

Of course, the strain is greater for those who have their mind attached to the Unmanifest, as attunement with the Unmanifest is attained with difficulty by the body-conscious people. (5)

ये तु सर्वाणि कर्माणि मयि सन्न्यस्य मत्पराः ।
अनन्येनैव योगेन मां ध्यायन्त उपासते ॥ ६ ॥

तेषामहं समुद्धर्ता मृत्युसंसारसागरात् ।
भवामि नचिरात्पार्थ मय्यावेशितचेतसाम् ॥ ७ ॥

On the other hand, those depending exclusively on Me, and surrendering all actions to Me, worship Me (God with attributes), constantly meditating on Me with single-minded devotion, them, Arjuna, I speedily deliver from the ocean of birth and death, their mind being fixed on Me. (6-7)

मय्येव मन आधत्स्व मयि बुद्धिं निवेशय ।
निवसिष्यसि मय्येव अत ऊर्ध्वं न संशयः ॥ ८ ॥

Therefore, fix your mind on Me, and establish

your intellect in Me alone; thereafter you will abide solely in Me. There is no doubt about it. (8)

अथ चित्तं समाधातुं न शक्नोषि मयि स्थिरम्।
अभ्यासयोगेन ततो मामिच्छाप्तुं धनञ्जय॥ ९॥

If you cannot steadily fix the mind on Me, Arjuna, then seek to attain Me through the Yoga of practice. (9)

अभ्यासेऽप्यसमर्थोऽसि मत्कर्मपरमो भव।
मदर्थमपि कर्माणि कुर्वन्सिद्धिमवाप्स्यसि॥ १०॥

If you are unequal even to the pursuit of such practice, be intent to work for Me; you shall attain perfection (in the form of My realization) even by performing actions for My sake. (10)

अथैतदप्यशक्तोऽसि कर्तुं मद्योगमाश्रितः।
सर्वकर्मफलत्यागं ततः कुरु यतात्मवान्॥ ११॥

If, taking recourse to the Yoga of My realization, you are unable even to do this, then, subduing your mind and intellect etc., relinquish the fruit of all actions. (11)

श्रेयो हि ज्ञानमभ्यासाज्ज्ञानाद्ध्यानं विशिष्यते।
ध्यानात्कर्मफलत्यागस्त्यागाच्छान्तिरनन्तरम्॥ १२॥

Knowledge is better than practice without discernment, meditation on God is superior to knowledge, and renunciation of the fruit of actions is even superior to meditation; for, peace immediately follows renunciation. (12)

अद्वेष्टा सर्वभूतानां मैत्रः करुण एव च।
निर्ममो निरहङ्कारः समदुःखसुखः क्षमी॥ १३॥

सन्तुष्टः सततं योगी यतात्मा दृढनिश्चयः।
मय्यर्पितमनोबुद्धिर्यो मद्भक्तः स मे प्रियः॥ १४॥

He who is free from malice towards all beings, friendly and compassionate, and free from the feelings of 'I' and 'mine', balanced in joy and sorrow, forgiving by nature, ever-contented and mentally united with Me, nay, who has subdued his mind, senses and body, has a firm resolve, and has surrendered his mind and reason to Me—that devotee of Mine is dear to Me.(13-14)

यस्मान्नोद्विजते लोको लोकान्नोद्विजते च यः।
हर्षामर्षभयोद्वेगैर्मुक्तो यः स च मे प्रियः॥ १५॥

He who is not a source of annoyance to his fellow-creatures, and who in his turn does not feel vexed with his fellow-creatures, and who is free from delight and envy, perturbation and fear, is dear to Me. (15)

अनपेक्षः शुचिर्दक्ष उदासीनो गतव्यथः।
सर्वारम्भपरित्यागी यो मद्भक्तः स मे प्रियः॥ १६॥

He who expects nothing, who is both internally and externally pure, is wise and impartial and has risen above all distractions, and who renounces the sense of doership in all undertakings—such a devotee of Mine is dear to Me. (16)

यो न हृष्यति न द्वेष्टि न शोचति न काङ्क्षति।
शुभाशुभपरित्यागी भक्तिमान्यः स मे प्रियः॥ १७॥

He who neither rejoices nor hates, nor grieves, nor desires, and who renounces both good and evil actions and is full of devotion, is dear to Me.(17)

समः शत्रौ च मित्रे च तथा मानापमानयोः।
शीतोष्णसुखदुःखेषु समः सङ्गविवर्जितः॥ १८॥
तुल्यनिन्दास्तुतिर्मौनी सन्तुष्टो येन केनचित्।
अनिकेतः स्थिरमतिर्भक्तिमान्मे प्रियो नरः॥ १९॥

He who deals equally with friend and foe, and is the same in honour and ignominy, who is alike in heat and cold, pleasure and pain and other contrary experiences, and is free from attachment, he who takes praise and reproach alike, and is given to contemplation and is contented with any means of subsistence available, entertaining no sense of ownership and attachment in respect of his dwelling-place and is full of devotion to Me, that person is dear to Me. (18-19)

ये तु धर्म्यामृतमिदं यथोक्तं पर्युपासते।
श्रद्दधाना मत्परमा भक्तास्तेऽतीव मे प्रियाः॥ २०॥

Those devotees, however, who partake in a disinterested way of this nectar of pious wisdom set forth above, endowed with faith and solely devoted to Me, they are extremely dear to Me. (20)

ॐ तत्सदिति श्रीमद्भगवद्गीतासूपनिषत्सु ब्रह्मविद्यायां
योगशास्त्रे श्रीकृष्णार्जुनसंवादे भक्तियोगो
नाम द्वादशोऽध्यायः॥ १२॥

Thus, in the Upaniṣad sung by the Lord, the Science of Brahma, the scripture of Yoga, the dialogue between Śrī Kṛṣṇa and Arjuna, ends the twelfth chapter entitled "The Yoga of Devotion."

Chapter XIII

श्रीभगवानुवाच

इदं शरीरं कौन्तेय क्षेत्रमित्यभिधीयते।
एतद्यो वेत्ति तं प्राहुः क्षेत्रज्ञ इति तद्विदः॥ १॥

Śrī Bhagavān said : This body, Arjuna is termed as the Field (Kṣetra) and he who knows it, is called the knower of the Field (Kṣetrajña) by the sages discerning the truth about both. (1)

क्षेत्रज्ञं चापि मां विद्धि सर्वक्षेत्रेषु भारत।
क्षेत्रक्षेत्रज्ञयोर्ज्ञानं यत्तज्ज्ञानं मतं मम॥ २॥

Know Myself to be the Kṣetrajña (individual soul) in all the Kṣetras (fields), Arjuna. And it is the knowledge of the field (Kṣetra) and knower (Kṣetrajña) (i.e., of Matter with its evolutes and the Spirit) which I consider as true knowledge. (2)

तत्क्षेत्रं यच्च यादृक्च यद्विकारि यतश्च यत्।
स च यो यत्प्रभावश्च तत्समासेन मे शृणु॥ ३॥

What that Field (Kṣetra) is and what is its nature, what are its modifications, and from what causes what effects have arisen, and also who its knower (Kṣetrajña) is, and what is His glory—hear all this from Me in brief. (3)

ऋषिभिर्बहुधा गीतं छन्दोभिर्विविधैः पृथक्।
ब्रह्मसूत्रपदैश्चैव हेतुमद्भिर्विनिश्चितैः ॥ ४ ॥

The truth about the Kṣetra and the Kṣetrajña has been expounded by the seers in manifold ways; again, it has been separately stated in different Vedic chants and also in the conclusive and reasoned texts of the Brahmasūtras. (4)

महाभूतान्यहङ्कारो बुद्धिरव्यक्तमेव च।
इन्द्रियाणि दशैकं च पञ्च चेन्द्रियगोचराः ॥ ५ ॥

The five elements, the ego, the intellect, the Unmanifest (Primordial Matter), the ten organs of perception and action, the mind, and the five objects of sense (sound, touch, colour, taste and smell). (5)

इच्छा द्वेषः सुखं दुःखं सङ्घातश्चेतना धृतिः।
एतत्क्षेत्रं समासेन सविकारमुदाहृतम् ॥ ६ ॥

Also desire, aversion, pleasure, pain, the physical body, consciousness, firmness: thus is the Kṣetra, with its evolutes, briefly stated. (6)

अमानित्वमदम्भित्वमहिंसा क्षान्तिरार्जवम्।
आचार्योपासनं शौचं स्थैर्यमात्मविनिग्रहः ॥ ७ ॥

Absence of pride, freedom from hypocrisy, non-violence, forbearance, uprightness of speech and mind etc., devout service of the preceptor, internal and external purity, steadfastness of mind and control of body, mind and the senses; (7)

इन्द्रियार्थेषु वैराग्यमनहङ्कार एव च।
जन्ममृत्युजराव्याधिदुःखदोषानुदर्शनम् ॥ ८ ॥

Dispassion towards the objects of enjoyment of this world and the next, and also absence of egotism, pondering again and again on the pain and evils inherent in birth, death, old age and disease; (8)

असक्तिरनभिष्वङ्गः पुत्रदारगृहादिषु।
नित्यं च समचित्तत्वमिष्टानिष्टोपपत्तिषु ॥ ९ ॥

Absence of attachment and the sense of mineness in respect of son, wife, home etc., and constant equipoise of mind both in favourable and unfavourable circumstances; (9)

मयि चानन्ययोगेन भक्तिरव्यभिचारिणी।
विविक्तदेशसेवित्वमरतिर्जनसंसदि ॥ १० ॥

Unflinching devotion to Me through exclusive attachment, living in secluded and holy places, and finding no delight in the company of worldly people; (10)

अध्यात्मज्ञाननित्यत्वं तत्त्वज्ञानार्थदर्शनम्।
एतज्ज्ञानमिति प्रोक्तमज्ञानं यदतोऽन्यथा ॥ ११ ॥

Constancy in self-knowledge and seeing God as the object of true knowledge—all this is declared as knowledge, and what is contrary to this is called ignorance. (11)

ज्ञेयं यत्तत्प्रवक्ष्यामि यज्ज्ञात्वामृतमश्नुते।
अनादिमत्परं ब्रह्म न सत्तन्नासदुच्यते॥ १२॥

I shall speak to you at length about that which ought to be known, and knowing which one attains supreme Bliss. That supreme Brahma, who is the lord of the two beginningless entities—Prakṛti and Jīva is said to be neither Sat (being) nor Asat (non-being).(12)

सर्वतः पाणिपादं तत्सर्वतोऽक्षिशिरोमुखम्।
सर्वतः श्रुतिमल्लोके सर्वमावृत्य तिष्ठति॥ १३॥

It has hands and feet on all sides, eyes, head and mouth in all directions, and ears all-round; for it stands pervading all in the universe. (13)

सर्वेन्द्रियगुणाभासं सर्वेन्द्रियविवर्जितम्।
असक्तं सर्वभृच्चैव निर्गुणं गुणभोक्तृ च॥ १४॥

Though perceiving all sense-objects, it is really speaking devoid of all senses. Nay, though unattached, it is the sustainer of all nonetheless; and though attributeless, it is the enjoyer of Guṇas, the three modes of Prakṛti. (14)

बहिरन्तश्च भूतानामचरं चरमेव च।
सूक्ष्मत्वात्तदविज्ञेयं दूरस्थं चान्तिके च तत्॥ १५॥

It exists without and within all beings, and constitutes the moving and the unmoving creation as well. And by reason of its subtlety, it is incomprehensible; it is close at hand and stands afar too. (15)

अविभक्तं च भूतेषु विभक्तमिव च स्थितम्।
भूतभर्तृ च तज्ज्ञेयं ग्रसिष्णु प्रभविष्णु च॥ १६॥

Though integral like space in its undivided aspect, it appears divided as it were, in all animate and inanimate beings. And that Godhead, which is the only object worth knowing, is the sustainer of beings (as Viṣṇu), the destroyer (as Rudra) and the creator of all (as Brahmā). (16)

ज्योतिषामपि तज्ज्योतिस्तमसः परमुच्यते।
ज्ञानं ज्ञेयं ज्ञानगम्यं हृदि सर्वस्य विष्ठितम्॥ १७॥

That supreme Brahma is said to be the light of all lights and entirely beyond Māyā. That godhead is knowledge itself, worth knowing, and worth attaining through real wisdom, and is particularly abiding in the hearts of all. (17)

इति क्षेत्रं तथा ज्ञानं ज्ञेयं चोक्तं समासतः।
मद्भक्त एतद्विज्ञाय मद्भावायोपपद्यते॥ १८॥

Thus the truth of the Kṣetra and knowledge, as well as of the object worth knowing, i.e., God, has been briefly discussed; knowing this in reality, My devotee attains to My being. (18)

प्रकृतिं पुरुषं चैव विद्ध्यनादी उभावपि।
विकारांश्च गुणांश्चैव विद्धि प्रकृतिसम्भवान्॥ १९॥

Prakṛti and Puruṣa, know both these as beginningless. And know all modifications such as likes and dislikes etc., and all objects constituted of the three Guṇas as born of Prakṛti. (19)

कार्यकरणकर्तृत्वे हेतुः प्रकृतिरुच्यते।
पुरुषः सुखदुःखानां भोक्तृत्वे हेतुरुच्यते॥ २०॥

Prakṛti is said to be responsible for bringing forth the evolutes and the instruments; while the individual soul is declared to be responsible for the experience of joys and sorrows. (20)

पुरुषः प्रकृतिस्थो हि भुङ्क्ते प्रकृतिजान्गुणान्।
कारणं गुणसङ्गोऽस्य सदसद्योनिजन्मसु॥ २१॥

Only the Puruṣa in association with Prakṛti experiences objects of the nature of the three Guṇas evolved from Prakṛti and it is attachment with these Guṇas that is responsible for the birth of this soul in good and evil wombs. (21)

उपद्रष्टानुमन्ता च भर्ता भोक्ता महेश्वरः।
परमात्मेति चाप्युक्तो देहेऽस्मिन्पुरुषः परः॥ २२॥

The Spirit dwelling in this body, is really the same as the Supreme. He has been spoken of as the Witness, the true Guide, the Sustainer of all, the Experiencer (as the embodied soul), the Overlord and the Absolute as well. (22)

य एवं वेत्ति पुरुषं प्रकृतिं च गुणैः सह।
सर्वथा वर्तमानोऽपि न स भूयोऽभिजायते॥ २३॥

He who thus knows the Puruṣa (Spirit) and Prakṛti (Nature) together with the Guṇas—even though performing his duties in everyway, is not born again. (23)

ध्यानेनात्मनि पश्यन्ति केचिदात्मानमात्मना।
अन्ये साङ्ख्येन योगेन कर्मयोगेन चापरे॥ २४॥

Some by meditation behold the supreme Spirit in the heart with the help of their refined and sharp intellect; others realize it through the discipline of Knowledge, and still others, through the discipline of Action, i.e., Karmayoga. (24)

अन्ये त्वेवमजानन्तः श्रुत्वान्येभ्य उपासते।
तेऽपि चातितरन्त्येव मृत्युं श्रुतिपरायणाः॥ २५॥

Other dull-witted persons, however, not knowing thus, worship even as they have heard from others i.e., the knowers of truth; and even those who are thus devoted to what they have heard, are able to cross the ocean of mundane existence in the shape of death.(25)

यावत्सञ्जायते किञ्चित्सत्त्वं स्थावरजङ्गमम्।
क्षेत्रक्षेत्रज्ञसंयोगात्तद्विद्धि भरतर्षभ॥ २६॥

Arjuna, whatsoever being, the moving or unmoving, is born, know it as emanated through the union of Kṣetra (Matter) and the Kṣetrajña (Spirit). (26)

समं सर्वेषु भूतेषु तिष्ठन्तं परमेश्वरम्।
विनश्यत्स्वविनश्यन्तं यः पश्यति स पश्यति॥ २७॥

He alone truly sees, who sees the supreme Lord

as imperishable and abiding equally in all perishable beings, both animate and inanimate. (27)

समं पश्यन्हि सर्वत्र समवस्थितमीश्वरम्।
न हिनस्त्यात्मनात्मानं ततो याति परां गतिम्॥ २८॥

For, by seeing the Supreme Lord equally present in all, he does not kill the Self by himself, and thereby attains the supreme state. (28)

प्रकृत्यैव च कर्माणि क्रियमाणानि सर्वशः।
यः पश्यति तथात्मानमकर्तारं स पश्यति॥ २९॥

He who sees that all actions are performed in everyway by nature (Prakṛti) and the Self as the non-doer, he alone verily sees. (29)

यदा भूतपृथग्भावमेकस्थमनुपश्यति।
तत एव च विस्तारं ब्रह्म सम्पद्यते तदा॥ ३०॥

The moment man perceives the diversified existence of beings as rooted in the one supreme Spirit, and the spreading forth of all beings from the same, that very moment he attains Brahma (who is Truth, Consciousness and Bliss solidified). (30)

अनादित्वान्निर्गुणत्वात्परमात्मायमव्ययः।
शरीरस्थोऽपि कौन्तेय न करोति न लिप्यते॥ ३१॥

Arjuna, being without beginning and without attributes, this indestructible supreme Spirit, though dwelling in the body, in fact does nothing, nor gets tainted. (31)

यथा सर्वगतं सौक्ष्म्यादाकाशं नोपलिप्यते।
सर्वत्रावस्थितो देहे तथात्मा नोपलिप्यते॥ ३२॥

As the all-pervading ether is not contaminated by reason of its subtlety, though permeating the body, the Self is not affected by the attributes of the body due to Its attributeless character. (32)

यथा प्रकाशयत्येकः कृत्स्नं लोकमिमं रविः।
क्षेत्रं क्षेत्री तथा कृत्स्नं प्रकाशयति भारत॥ ३३॥

Arjuna, as the one sun illumines this entire universe, so the one Ātmā (Spirit) illumines the whole Kṣetra (Field). (33)

क्षेत्रक्षेत्रज्ञयोरेवमन्तरं ज्ञानचक्षुषा।
भूतप्रकृतिमोक्षं च ये विदुर्यान्ति ते परम्॥ ३४॥

Those who thus perceive with the eye of wisdom, the difference between the Kṣetra and Kṣetrajña, and the phenomenon of liberation from Prakṛti with her evolutes, reach the supreme eternal Spirit. (34)

ॐ तत्सदिति श्रीमद्भगवद्गीतासूपनिषत्सु ब्रह्मविद्यायां
योगशास्त्रे श्रीकृष्णार्जुनसंवादे क्षेत्रक्षेत्रज्ञविभागयोगो
नाम त्रयोदशोऽध्यायः॥ १३॥

Thus, in the Upaniṣad sung by the Lord, the Science of Brahma, the scripture of Yoga, the dialogue between Śrī Kṛṣṇa and Arjuna, ends the thirteenth chapter entitled "The Yoga of discrimination between the Field and the Knower of the Field."

Chapter XIV

श्रीभगवानुवाच

परं भूयः प्रवक्ष्यामि ज्ञानानां ज्ञानमुत्तमम्।
यज्ज्ञात्वा मुनयः सर्वे परां सिद्धिमितो गताः॥ १॥

Śrī Bhagavān said : I shall expound once more the supreme knowledge, the best of all knowledge, acquiring which all sages have attained highest perfection, being liberated from this mundane existence. (1)

इदं ज्ञानमुपाश्रित्य मम साधर्म्यमागताः।
सर्गेऽपि नोपजायन्ते प्रलये न व्यथन्ति च॥ २॥

Those who, by practising this knowledge have entered into My being, are not born again at the cosmic dawn, nor feel disturbed even during the cosmic dissolution (Pralaya). (2)

मम योनिर्महद्ब्रह्म तस्मिन्गर्भं दधाम्यहम्।
सम्भवः सर्वभूतानां ततो भवति भारत॥ ३॥

My primordial Nature, known as the great Brahma, is the womb of all creatures; in that womb I place the seed of all life. The creation of all beings follows from that union of Matter and Spirit, O Arjuna. (3)

सर्वयोनिषु कौन्तेय मूर्तयः सम्भवन्ति याः।
तासां ब्रह्म महद्योनिरहं बीजप्रदः पिता॥ ४॥

Of all embodied beings that appear in all the species of various kinds, Arjuna, Prakṛti or Nature is the conceiving Mother, while I am the seed-giving Father. (4)

सत्त्वं रजस्तम इति गुणाः प्रकृतिसम्भवाः।
निबध्नन्ति महाबाहो देहे देहिनमव्ययम्॥ ५॥

Sattva, Rajas and Tamas—these three Guṇas born of Nature tie down the imperishable soul to the body, Arjuna. (5)

तत्र सत्त्वं निर्मलत्वात्प्रकाशकमनामयम्।
सुखसङ्गेन बध्नाति ज्ञानसङ्गेन चानघ॥ ६॥

Of these, Sattva being immaculate, is illuminating and flawless, Arjuna; it binds through attachment to happiness and knowledge. (6)

रजो रागात्मकं विद्धि तृष्णासङ्गसमुद्भवम्।
तन्निबध्नाति कौन्तेय कर्मसङ्गेन देहिनम्॥ ७॥

Arjuna, know the quality of Rajas, which is of the nature of passion, as born of desire and attachment. It binds the soul through attachment to actions and their fruit. (7)

तमस्त्वज्ञानजं विद्धि मोहनं सर्वदेहिनाम्।
प्रमादालस्यनिद्राभिस्तन्निबध्नाति भारत॥ ८॥

And know Tamas, the deluder of all those who

look upon the body as their own self, as born of ignorance. It binds the soul through error, sleep and sloth, Arjuna. (8)

सत्त्वं सुखे सञ्जयति रजः कर्मणि भारत।
ज्ञानमावृत्य तु तमः प्रमादे सञ्जयत्युत॥ ९ ॥

Sattva draws one to joy and Rajas to action; while Tamas, clouding wisdom, impels one to error, sleep and sloth Arjuna. (9)

रजस्तमश्चाभिभूय सत्त्वं भवति भारत।
रजः सत्त्वं तमश्चैव तमः सत्त्वं रजस्तथा॥ १० ॥

Overpowering Rajas and Tamas, Arjuna, Sattva prevails; overpowering Sattva and Tamas, Rajas prevails; even so, overpowering Sattva and Rajas, Tamas prevails. (10)

सर्वद्वारेषु देहेऽस्मिन्प्रकाश उपजायते।
ज्ञानं यदा तदा विद्याद्विवृद्धं सत्त्वमित्युत॥ ११ ॥

When light and discernment dawn in this body, as well as in the mind and senses, then one should know that Sattva is predominant. (11)

लोभः प्रवृत्तिरारम्भः कर्मणामशमः स्पृहा।
रजस्येतानि जायन्ते विवृद्धे भरतर्षभ॥ १२ ॥

With the preponderance of Rajas, Arjuna, greed, activity, undertaking of action with an interested motive, restlessness and a thirst for enjoyment make their appearance. (12)

अप्रकाशोऽप्रवृत्तिश्च प्रमादो मोह एव च।
तमस्येतानि जायन्ते विवृद्धे कुरुनन्दन॥ १३॥

With the growth of Tamas, Arjuna, obtuseness of the mind and senses, disinclination to perform one's obligatory duties, frivolity and stupor—all these appear. (13)

यदा सत्त्वे प्रवृद्धे तु प्रलयं याति देहभृत्।
तदोत्तमविदां लोकानमलान्प्रतिपद्यते॥ १४॥

When a man dies during the preponderance of Sattva, he obtains the stainless ethereal worlds (heaven etc.,) attained by men of noble deeds.(14)

रजसि प्रलयं गत्वा कर्मसङ्गिषु जायते।
तथा प्रलीनस्तमसि मूढयोनिषु जायते॥ १५॥

Dying when Rajas predominates, he is born among those attached to action; even so, the man who has expired during the preponderance of Tamas is reborn in the species of the deluded creatures such as insects and beasts etc. (15)

कर्मणः सुकृतस्याहुः सात्त्विकं निर्मलं फलम्।
रजसस्तु फलं दुःखमज्ञानं तमसः फलम्॥ १६॥

The reward of a righteous act, they say, is Sāttvika i.e., faultless in the form of joy, wisdom and dispassion etc., sorrow is declared to be the fruit of a Rājasika act and ignorance, the fruit of a Tāmasika act. (16)

सत्त्वात्सञ्जायते ज्ञानं रजसो लोभ एव च।
प्रमादमोहौ तमसो भवतोऽज्ञानमेव च॥ १७॥

Wisdom follows from Sattva, and greed, undoubtedly, from Rajas; likewise, obstinate error, stupor and also ignorance follow from Tamas. (17)

ऊर्ध्वं गच्छन्ति सत्त्वस्था मध्ये तिष्ठन्ति राजसाः।
जघन्यगुणवृत्तिस्था अधो गच्छन्ति तामसाः॥ १८॥

Those who abide in the quality of Sattva wend their way upwards; while those of a Rājasika disposition stay in the middle. And those of a Tāmasika temperament, enveloped as they are in the effects of Tamoguṇa, sink down. (18)

नान्यं गुणेभ्यः कर्तारं यदा द्रष्टानुपश्यति।
गुणेभ्यश्च परं वेत्ति मद्भावं सोऽधिगच्छति॥ १९॥

When the discerning person sees no one as doer other than the three Guṇas, and realizes Me, the supreme Spirit standing entirely beyond these Guṇas, he enters into My being. (19)

गुणानेतानतीत्य त्रीन्देही देहसमुद्भवान्।
जन्ममृत्युजरादुःखैर्विमुक्तोऽमृतमश्नुते॥ २०॥

Having transcended the aforesaid three Guṇas, which have caused the body, and freed from birth, death, old age and all kinds of sorrow, the embodied soul attains supreme bliss. (20)

अर्जुन उवाच

कैर्लिङ्गैस्त्रीन्गुणानेतानतीतो भवति प्रभो।
किमाचारः कथं चैतांस्त्रीन्गुणानतिवर्तते॥ २१॥

Arjuna said : What are the marks of him who

has risen above the three Guṇas, and what is his conduct ? And how, Lord, does he rise above the three Guṇas? (21)

श्रीभगवानुवाच

प्रकाशं च प्रवृत्तिं च मोहमेव च पाण्डव।
न द्वेष्टि सम्प्रवृत्तानि न निवृत्तानि काङ्क्षति॥ २२॥

Śrī Bhagavān said: Arjuna, he who abhorsh not illumination (which is born of Sattva) and activity (which is born of Rajas) and even stupor (which is born of Tamas), when prevalent, nor longs for them when they have ceased. (22)

उदासीनवदासीनो गुणैर्यो न विचाल्यते।
गुणा वर्तन्त इत्येव योऽवतिष्ठति नेङ्गते॥ २३॥

He who, sitting like a witness, is not disturbed by the Guṇas, and who, knowing that the Guṇas alone move among the Guṇas, remains established in identity with God, and never falls off from that state. (23)

समदुःखसुखः स्वस्थः समलोष्टाश्मकाञ्चनः।
तुल्यप्रियाप्रियो धीरस्तुल्यनिन्दात्मसंस्तुतिः॥ २४॥

He who is ever established in the Self, takes pain and pleasure alike, regards a clod of earth, a stone and a piece of gold as equal in value, is possessed of wisdom, accepts the pleasant as well as the unpleasant in the same spirit, and views censure and praise alike. (24)

मानापमानयोस्तुल्यस्तुल्यो मित्रारिपक्षयोः।
सर्वारम्भपरित्यागी गुणातीतः स उच्यते॥ २५॥

He who is equipoised in honour or ignominy, is alike towards a friend or an enemy, and has renounced the sense of doership in all undertakings, is said to have risen above the three Guṇas.(25)

मां च योऽव्यभिचारेण भक्तियोगेन सेवते।
स गुणान्समतीत्यैतान्ब्रह्मभूयाय कल्पते॥ २६॥

He too who, constantly worships Me through the Yoga of exclusive devotion—transcending these three Guṇas, he becomes eligible for attaining Brahma. (26)

ब्रह्मणो हि प्रतिष्ठाहममृतस्याव्ययस्य च।
शाश्वतस्य च धर्मस्य सुखस्यैकान्तिकस्य च॥ २७॥

For, I am the substratum of the imperishable Brahma, of immortality, of the eternal Dharma and of unending immutable bliss. (27)

ॐ तत्सदिति श्रीमद्भगवद्गीतासूपनिषत्सु ब्रह्मविद्यायां
योगशास्त्रे श्रीकृष्णार्जुनसंवादे गुणत्रयविभागयोगो
नाम चतुर्दशोऽध्यायः॥ १४॥

Thus, in the Upaniṣad sung by the Lord, the Science of Brahma, the scripture of Yoga, the dialogue between Śrī Kṛṣṇa and Arjuna, ends the fourteenth chapter entitled "The Yoga of Division of three Guṇas."

Chapter XV

श्रीभगवानुवाच

ऊर्ध्वमूलमधःशाखमश्वत्थं प्राहुरव्ययम्।
छन्दांसि यस्य पर्णानि यस्तं वेद स वेदवित्॥ १॥

Śrī Bhagavān said : He who knows the Pīpala tree (in the form of creation); which is said to be imperishable with its roots in the Primeval Being (God), whose branch is represented by Brahmā (the Creator), and whose leaves are the Vedas, is a knower of the purport of the Vedas. (1)

अधश्चोर्ध्वं प्रसृतास्तस्य शाखा
गुणप्रवृद्धा विषयप्रवालाः।
अधश्च मूलान्यनुसन्ततानि
कर्मानुबन्धीनि मनुष्यलोके॥ २॥

Fed by the three Guṇas and having sense-objects for their tender leaves, the branches of the aforesaid tree (in the shape of the different orders of creation) extend both downwards and upwards; and its roots, which bind the soul according to its actions in the human body, are spread in all regions, higher as well as lower. (2)

न रूपमस्येह तथोपलभ्यते
नान्तो न चादिर्न च सम्प्रतिष्ठा।
अश्वत्थमेनं सुविरूढमूल-
मसङ्गशस्त्रेण दृढेन छित्त्वा॥ ३॥

The nature of this tree of creation, does not on mature thought, turn out what it is represented to be; for it has neither beginning nor end, nor even stability. Therefore, cutting down this Pīpala tree, which is most firmly rooted, with the formidable axe of dispassion. (3)

ततः पदं तत्परिमार्गितव्यं-
यस्मिन्गता न निवर्तन्ति भूयः।
तमेव चाद्यं पुरुषं प्रपद्ये
यतः प्रवृत्तिः प्रसृता पुराणी॥ ४॥

Thereafter a man should diligently seek for that supreme state, viz., God, having attained which they return no more to this world; and having fully resolved that he stands dedicated to that Primeval Being (God Nārāyaṇa) Himself, from whom the flow of this beginningless creation has progressed, he should dwell and meditate on Him. (4)

निर्मानमोहा जितसङ्गदोषा
अध्यात्मनित्या विनिवृत्तकामाः।

द्वन्द्वैर्विमुक्ताः सुखदुःखसञ्ज्ञै-
र्गच्छन्त्यमूढाः पदमव्ययं तत्॥ ५ ॥

They who are free from pride and delusion, who have conquered the evil of attachment, and are constantly abiding in God, whose cravings have altogether ceased and who are completely immune to all pairs of opposites going by the names of pleasure and pain, and are undeluded, attain that supreme immortal state. (5)

न तद्भासयते सूर्यो न शशाङ्को न पावकः।
यद्गत्वा न निवर्तन्ते तद्धाम परमं मम॥ ६ ॥

Neither the sun nor the moon nor fire can illumine that supreme self-effulgent state, attaining which they never return to this world; that is My supreme abode. (6)

ममैवांशो जीवलोके जीवभूतः सनातनः।
मनःषष्ठानीन्द्रियाणि प्रकृतिस्थानि कर्षति॥ ७ ॥

The eternal Jīvātmā in this body is a fragment of My own Self; and it is that alone which draws around itself the mind and the five senses, which abide in Prakṛti. (7)

शरीरं यदवाप्नोति यच्चाप्युत्क्रामतीश्वरः।
गृहीत्वैतानि संयाति वायुर्गन्धानिवाशयात्॥ ८ ॥

Even as the wind wafts scents from their seat, so, too, the Jīvātmā, which is the controller of the body etc., taking the mind and the senses from the body which it leaves behind, forthwith migrates to the body which it acquires. (8)

श्रोत्रं चक्षुः स्पर्शनं च रसनं घ्राणमेव च।
अधिष्ठाय मनश्चायं विषयानुपसेवते॥ ९ ॥

It is while dwelling in the senses of hearing, sight, touch, taste and smell, as well as in the mind, that this Jīvātmā enjoys the objects of senses. (9)

उत्क्रामन्तं स्थितं वापि भुञ्जानं वा गुणान्वितम्।
विमूढा नानुपश्यन्ति पश्यन्ति ज्ञानचक्षुषः॥ १० ॥

The ignorant know not the soul departing from, or dwelling in the body, or enjoying the objects of senses, i.e., even when it is connected with the three Guṇas; only those endowed with the eyes of wisdom are able to realize it. (10)

यतन्तो योगिनश्चैनं पश्यन्त्यात्मन्यवस्थितम्।
यतन्तोऽप्यकृतात्मानो नैनं पश्यन्त्यचेतसः॥ ११ ॥

Striving Yogīs too are able to realise this Self enshrined in their heart. The ignorant, however, whose heart has not been purified, know not this Self in spite of their best endeavours. (11)

यदादित्यगतं तेजो जगद्भासयतेऽखिलम्।
यच्चन्द्रमसि यच्चाग्नौ तत्तेजो विद्धि मामकम्॥ १२॥

The radiance in the sun that illumines the entire world, and that which shines in the moon and that which shines in the fire too, know that radiance to be Mine. (12)

गामाविश्य च भूतानि धारयाम्यहमोजसा।
पुष्णामि चौषधीः सर्वाः सोमो भूत्वा रसात्मकः॥ १३॥

And permeating the soil, it is I who support all creatures by My vital energy, and becoming the sapful moon, I nourish all plants. (13)

अहं वैश्वानरो भूत्वा प्राणिनां देहमाश्रितः।
प्राणापानसमायुक्तः पचाम्यन्नं चतुर्विधम्॥ १४॥

Taking the form of fire, as Vaiśvānara, lodged in the body of all creatures and united with the Prāṇa (exhalation) and Apāna (inhalation) breaths, it is I who digest and assimilate the four kinds of food. (14)

सर्वस्य चाहं हृदि सन्निविष्टो
मत्तः स्मृतिर्ज्ञानमपोहनं च।
वेदैश्च सर्वैरहमेव वेद्यो-
वेदान्तकृद्वेदविदेव चाहम्॥ १५॥

It is I who remain seated in the heart of all

creatures as the inner controller of all; and it is I who am the source of memory, knowledge and the ratiocinative faculty. Again, I am the only object worth knowing through the Vedas; I alone am the origin of Vedānta and the knower of the Vedas too. (15)

द्वाविमौ पुरुषौ लोके क्षरश्चाक्षर एव च।
क्षरः सर्वाणि भूतानि कूटस्थोऽक्षर उच्यते॥ १६॥

The perishable and the imperishable too—these are the two kinds of Puruṣas in this world. Of these, the bodies of all beings are spoken of as the perishable; while the Jīvātmā or the embodied soul is called imperishable. (16)

उत्तमः पुरुषस्त्वन्यः परमात्मेत्युदाहृतः।
यो लोकत्रयमाविश्य बिभर्त्यव्यय ईश्वरः॥ १७॥

Yet, the Supreme Person is other than these, who, having encompassed all the three worlds, upholds and maintains all, and has been spoken of as the imperishable Lord and the Supreme Spirit. (17)

यस्मात्क्षरमतीतोऽहमक्षरादपि चोत्तमः।
अतोऽस्मि लोके वेदे च प्रथितः पुरुषोत्तमः॥ १८॥

Since I am wholly beyond the perishable world of matter or Kṣetra, and am superior even to the imperishable soul, Jīvātmā, hence I am known as the Puruṣottama, the Supreme Self, in the world as well as in the Vedas. (18)

यो मामेवमसम्मूढो जानाति पुरुषोत्तमम्।
स सर्वविद्भजति मां सर्वभावेन भारत॥ १९॥

Arjuna, the wise man who thus realizes Me as the Supreme Person—knowing all, he constantly worships Me (the all-pervading Lord) with his whole being. (19)

इति गुह्यतमं शास्त्रमिदमुक्तं मयानघ।
एतद्बुद्ध्वा बुद्धिमान्स्यात्कृतकृत्यश्च भारत॥ २०॥

Arjuna, this most esoteric teaching has thus been imparted by Me; grasping it in essence man becomes wise and his mission in life is accomplished.(20)

ॐ तत्सदिति श्रीमद्भगवद्गीतासूपनिषत्सु ब्रह्मविद्यायां
योगशास्त्रे श्रीकृष्णार्जुनसंवादे पुरुषोत्तमयोगो
नाम पञ्चदशोऽध्यायः॥ १५॥

Thus, in the Upaniṣad sung by the Lord, the Science of Brahma, the scripture of Yoga, the dialogue between Śrī Kṛṣṇa and Arjuna, ends the fifteenth chapter entitled "The Yoga of the Supreme Person."

Chapter XVI

श्रीभगवानुवाच

अभयं सत्त्वसंशुद्धिर्ज्ञानयोगव्यवस्थितिः।
दानं दमश्च यज्ञश्च स्वाध्यायस्तप आर्जवम्॥ १॥

Absolute fearlessness, perfect purity of mind, constant fixity in the Yoga of meditation for the sake of Self-realization, and even so, charity in its Sāttvika form, control of the senses, worship of God and other deities as well as of one's elders including the performance of Agnihotra (pouring oblations into the sacred fire) and other sacred duties, study and teaching of the Vedas and other sacred books as well as the chanting of God's names and glories, suffering hardships for the discharge of one's sacred obligations and uprightness of mind as well as of the body and senses. (1)

अहिंसा सत्यमक्रोधस्त्यागः शान्तिरपैशुनम्।
दया भूतेष्वलोलुप्त्वं मार्दवं ह्रीरचापलम्॥ २॥

Non-violence in thought, word and deed, truthfulness and geniality of speech, absence of anger even on provocation, disclaiming doership in respect of actions, quietude or composure of mind, abstaining from slander, compassion towards all creatures, absence of attachment to the objects of senses even during their contact with the senses, mildness, a sense of shame in transgressing the scriptures or social conventions, and abstaining from frivolous pursuits; (2)

तेजः क्षमा धृतिः शौचमद्रोहो नातिमानिता।
भवन्ति सम्पदं दैवीमभिजातस्य भारत॥ ३॥

Sublimity, forgiveness, fortitude, external purity, bearing enmity to none and absence of self-esteem—these are, O Arjuna, the marks of him, who is born with the divine endowments. (3)

दम्भो दर्पोऽभिमानश्च क्रोधः पारुष्यमेव च।
अज्ञानं चाभिजातस्य पार्थ सम्पदमासुरीम्॥ ४॥

Hypocrisy, arrogance, pride and anger, sternness and ignorance too—these are, the marks of him, who is born with demoniac properties. (4)

दैवी सम्पद्विमोक्षाय निबन्धायासुरी मता।
मा शुचः सम्पदं दैवीमभिजातोऽसि पाण्डव॥ ५॥

The divine endowment has been recognized as conducive to liberation, and the demoniac one as leading to bondage. Grieve not, Arjuna, for you are born with the divine propensities. (5)

द्वौ भूतसर्गौ लोकेऽस्मिन्दैव आसुर एव च।
दैवो विस्तरशः प्रोक्त आसुरं पार्थ मे शृणु॥ ६॥

There are only two types of men in this world,

Arjuna, the one possessing a divine nature and the other possessing a demoniac disposition. Of these, the type possessing divine nature has been dealt with at length; now hear in detail from Me about the type possessing demoniac disposition. (6)

प्रवृत्तिं च निवृत्तिं च जना न विदुरासुराः।
न शौचं नापि चाचारो न सत्यं तेषु विद्यते॥ ७॥

Men possessing a demoniac disposition know not what is right activity and what is right abstinence from activity. Hence they possess neither purity (external or internal) nor good conduct nor even truthfulness. (7)

असत्यमप्रतिष्ठं ते जगदाहुरनीश्वरम्।
अपरस्परसम्भूतं किमन्यत्कामहैतुकम्॥ ८॥

Men of demoniac disposition say this world is without any foundation, absolutely unreal and Godless, brought forth by mutual union of the male and female and hence conceived in lust; what else than this? (8)

एतां दृष्टिमवष्टभ्य नष्टात्मानोऽल्पबुद्धयः।
प्रभवन्त्युग्रकर्माणः क्षयाय जगतोऽहिताः॥ ९॥

Clinging to this false view these slow-witted men of vile disposition and terrible deeds, are enemies of mankind, bent on destruction of the world. (9)

काममाश्रित्य दुष्पूरं दम्भमानमदान्विताः।
मोहाद्गृहीत्वासद्ग्राहान्प्रवर्तन्तेऽशुचिव्रताः ॥ १० ॥

Cherishing insatiable desires and embracing false doctrines through ignorance, these men of impure conduct move in this world, full of hypocrisy, pride and arrogance. (10)

चिन्तामपरिमेयां च प्रलयान्तामुपाश्रिताः।
कामोपभोगपरमा एतावदिति निश्चिताः ॥ ११ ॥

Giving themselves up to innumerable cares ending only with death, they remain devoted to the enjoyment of sensuous pleasures and are firm in their belief that this is the highest limit of joy. (11)

आशापाशशतैर्बद्धाः कामक्रोधपरायणाः।
ईहन्ते कामभोगार्थमन्यायेनार्थसञ्चयान् ॥ १२ ॥

Held in bondage by hundreds of ties of expectation and wholly giving themselves up to lust and anger, they strive to amass by unfair means hoards of money and other objects for the enjoyment of sensuous pleasures. (12)

इदमद्य मया लब्धमिमं प्राप्स्ये मनोरथम्।
इदमस्तीदमपि मे भविष्यति पुनर्धनम् ॥ १३ ॥

They say to themselves, "This much has been secured by me today and now I shall realize this ambition. So much wealth is already with me and yet again this shall be mine. (13)

असौ मया हतः शत्रुर्हनिष्ये चापरानपि।
ईश्वरोऽहमहं भोगी सिद्धोऽहं बलवान्सुखी॥ १४॥

That enemy has been slain by me and I shall kill those others too. I am the lord of all, the enjoyer of all power, I am endowed with all occult powers, and am mighty and happy. (14)

आढ्योऽभिजनवानस्मि कोऽन्योऽस्ति सदृशो मया।
यक्ष्ये दास्यामि मोदिष्य इत्यज्ञानविमोहिताः॥ १५॥
अनेकचित्तविभ्रान्ता मोहजालसमावृताः।
प्रसक्ताः कामभोगेषु पतन्ति नरकेऽशुचौ॥ १६॥

"I am wealthy and own a large family; who else is equal to me? I will sacrifice to gods, will give alms, I will make merry," Thus deluded by ignorance, enveloped in the mesh of delusion and addicted to the enjoyment of sensuous pleasures, their mind bewildered by numerous thoughts, these men of devilish disposition fall into the foulest hell. (15-16)

आत्मसम्भाविताः स्तब्धा धनमानमदान्विताः।
यजन्ते नामयज्ञैस्ते दम्भेनाविधिपूर्वकम्॥ १७॥

Intoxicated by wealth and honour, those self-conceited and haughty men perform sacrifices only in name for ostentation, without following the sacred rituals. (17)

अहङ्कारं बलं दर्पं कामं क्रोधं च संश्रिताः।
मामात्मपरदेहेषु प्रद्विषन्तोऽभ्यसूयकाः॥ १८॥

Given over to egotism, brute force, arrogance, lust and anger etc., and calumniating others, they despise Me (the in-dweller), dwelling in their own bodies, as in those of others. (18)

तानहं द्विषतः क्रूरान्संसारेषु नराधमान्।
क्षिपाम्यजस्रमशुभानासुरीष्वेव योनिषु॥ १९॥

Those haters, sinful, cruel and vilest among men, I cast again and again into demoniacal wombs in this world. (19)

आसुरीं योनिमापन्ना मूढा जन्मनि जन्मनि।
मामप्राप्यैव कौन्तेय ततो यान्त्यधमां गतिम्॥ २०॥

Failing to reach Me, Arjuna, those stupid persons are born life after life in demoniac wombs and then verily sink down to a still lower plane.(20)

त्रिविधं नरकस्येदं द्वारं नाशनमात्मनः।
कामः क्रोधस्तथा लोभस्तस्मादेतत्त्रयं त्यजेत्॥ २१॥

Desire, anger and greed—these triple gates of hell, bring about the downfall of the soul. Therefore, one should shun all these three. (21)

एतैर्विमुक्तः कौन्तेय तमोद्वारैस्त्रिभिर्नरः।
आचरत्यात्मनः श्रेयस्ततो याति परां गतिम्॥ २२॥

Freed from these three gates of hell, man works

for his own salvation and thereby attains the supreme goal, i.e., God. (22)

यः शास्त्रविधिमुत्सृज्य वर्तते कामकारतः।
न स सिद्धिमवाप्नोति न सुखं न परां गतिम्॥ २३॥

Discarding the injunctions of the scriptures, he who acts in an arbitrary way according to his own sweet will, such a person neither attains occult powers, nor the supreme goal, nor even happiness. (23)

तस्माच्छास्त्रं प्रमाणं ते कार्याकार्यव्यवस्थितौ।
ज्ञात्वा शास्त्रविधानोक्तं कर्म कर्तुमिहार्हसि॥ २४॥

Therefore, the scripture alone is your guide in determining what should be done and what should not be done. Knowing this, you ought to perform only such action as is ordained by the scriptures. (24)

ॐ तत्सदिति श्रीमद्भगवद्गीतासूपनिषत्सु ब्रह्मविद्यायां
योगशास्त्रे श्रीकृष्णार्जुनसंवादे दैवासुरसम्पद्विभागयोगो
नाम षोडशोऽध्यायः॥ १६॥

Thus, in the Upaniṣad sung by the Lord, the Science of Brahma, the scripture of Yoga, the dialogue between Śrī Kṛṣṇa and Arjuna, ends the sixteenth chapter entitled "The Yoga of Division between the Divine and the Demoniacal Properties."

Chapter XVII

अर्जुन उवाच

ये शास्त्रविधिमुत्सृज्य यजन्ते श्रद्धयान्विताः।
तेषां निष्ठा तु का कृष्ण सत्त्वमाहो रजस्तमः॥ १॥

Arjuna said: Those, endowed with faith, who worship gods and others, disregarding the injunctions of the scriptures, where do they stand, Kṛṣṇa—in Sattva, Rajas or Tamas? (1)

श्रीभगवानुवाच

त्रिविधा भवति श्रद्धा देहिनां सा स्वभावजा।
सात्त्विकी राजसी चैव तामसी चेति तां शृणु॥ २॥

Śrī Bhagavān said: That untutored innate faith of men is of three kinds—Sāttvika, Rājasika and Tāmasika. Hear of it from Me. (2)

सत्त्वानुरूपा सर्वस्य श्रद्धा भवति भारत।
श्रद्धामयोऽयं पुरुषो यो यच्छ्रद्धः स एव सः॥ ३॥

The faith of all men conforms to their mental disposition, Arjuna. Faith constitutes a man; whatever the nature of his faith, verily he is that. (3)

यजन्ते सात्त्विका देवान्यक्षरक्षांसि राजसाः।
प्रेतान्भूतगणांश्चान्ये यजन्ते तामसा जनाः॥ ४॥

Men of Sāttvika disposition worship gods; those of Rājasika temperament worship demigods, the demons; while others, who are of Tāmasika disposition, worship the spirits of the dead and ghosts. (4)

अशास्त्रविहितं घोरं तप्यन्ते ये तपो जनाः।
दम्भाहङ्कारसंयुक्ताः कामरागबलान्विताः॥ ५॥

Men who practise severe penance of an arbitrary type, not sanctioned by the scriptures, and who are full of hypocrisy and egotism and are obsessed with desire, attachment and pride of power; (5)

कर्शयन्तः शरीरस्थं भूतग्राममचेतसः।
मां चैवान्तः शरीरस्थं तान्विद्ध्यासुरनिश्चयान्॥ ६॥

And who emaciate the elements constituting their body as well as Me, the Supreme Spirit, dwelling in their heart—know those senseless people to have a demoniac disposition. (6)

आहारस्त्वपि सर्वस्य त्रिविधो भवति प्रियः।
यज्ञस्तपस्तथा दानं तेषां भेदमिमं शृणु॥ ७॥

Food also, which is agreeable to different men according to their innate disposition is of three kinds. And, likewise, sacrifice, penance and charity too are of three kinds each; hear their distinction as follows. (7)

आयुःसत्त्वबलारोग्यसुखप्रीतिविवर्धनाः ।
रस्याः स्निग्धाः स्थिरा हृद्या आहाराः सात्त्विकप्रियाः ॥ ८ ॥

Foods which promote longevity, intelligence, vigour, health, happiness and cheerfulness, and which are juicy, succulent, substantial and naturally agreeable, are liked by men of Sāttvika nature. (8)

कट्वम्ललवणात्युष्णतीक्ष्णरूक्षविदाहिनः ।
आहारा राजसस्येष्टा दुःखशोकामयप्रदाः ॥ ९ ॥

Foods which are bitter, sour, salty, overhot, pungent, dry and burning, and which cause suffering, grief and sickness, are dear to the Rājasika. (9)

यातयामं गतरसं पूति पर्युषितं च यत् ।
उच्छिष्टमपि चामेध्यं भोजनं तामसप्रियम् ॥ १० ॥

Food which is ill-cooked or not fully ripe, insipid, putrid, stale and polluted, and which is impure too, is dear to men of Tāmasika disposition. (10)

अफलाकाङ्क्षिभिर्यज्ञो विधिदृष्टो य इज्यते ।
यष्टव्यमेवेति मनः समाधाय स सात्त्विकः ॥ ११ ॥

The sacrifice which is offered, as ordained by

scriptural injunctions, by men who expect no return and who believe that such sacrifices must be performed, is Sāttvika in character. (11)

अभिसन्धाय तु फलं दम्भार्थमपि चैव यत्।
इज्यते भरतश्रेष्ठ तं यज्ञं विद्धि राजसम्॥ १२॥

That sacrifice, however, which is offered for the sake of mere show or even with an eye to its fruit, know it to be Rājasika, Arjuna. (12)

विधिहीनमसृष्टान्नं मन्त्रहीनमदक्षिणम्।
श्रद्धाविरहितं यज्ञं तामसं परिचक्षते॥ १३॥

A sacrifice, which is not in conformity with scriptural injunctions, in which no food is offered, and no sacrificial fees are paid, which is without sacred chant of hymns and devoid of faith, is said to be Tāmasika. (13)

देवद्विजगुरुप्राज्ञपूजनं शौचमार्जवम्।
ब्रह्मचर्यमहिंसा च शारीरं तप उच्यते॥ १४॥

Worship of gods, the Brāhmaṇas, one's guru, elders and great soul, purity, straightforwardness, continence and non-violence—these are called penance of the body. (14)

अनुद्वेगकरं वाक्यं सत्यं प्रियहितं च यत्।
स्वाध्यायाभ्यसनं चैव वाङ्मयं तप उच्यते॥ १५॥

Words which cause no annoyance to others

and are truthful, agreeable and beneficial, as well as the study of the Vedas and other Śāstras and the practice of the chanting of Divine Name—this is known as penance of speech. (15)

मनःप्रसादः सौम्यत्वं मौनमात्मविनिग्रहः।
भावसंशुद्धिरित्येतत्तपो मानसमुच्यते॥ १६॥

Cheerfulness of mind, placidity, habit of contemplation on God, control of the mind and perfect purity of inner feelings—all this is called austerity of the mind. (16)

श्रद्धया परया तप्तं तपस्तत्त्रिविधं नरैः।
अफलाकाङ्क्षिभिर्युक्तैः सात्त्विकं परिचक्षते॥ १७॥

This threefold penance performed with supreme faith by Yogīs expecting no return is called Sāttvika. (17)

सत्कारमानपूजार्थं तपो दम्भेन चैव यत्।
क्रियते तदिह प्रोक्तं राजसं चलमध्रुवम्॥ १८॥

The austerity which is performed for the sake of renown, honour or adoration, as well as for any other selfish gain, either in all sincerity or by way of ostentation, and yields an uncertain and momentary fruit, has been spoken of here as Rājasika. (18)

मूढग्राहेणात्मनो यत्पीडया क्रियते तपः।
परस्योत्सादनार्थं वा तत्तामसमुदाहृतम्॥ १९॥

Penance which is resorted to out of foolish obstinacy and is accompanied by self-mortification, or is intended to harm others, such penance has been declared as Tāmasika. (19)

दातव्यमिति यद्दानं दीयतेऽनुपकारिणे।
देशे काले च पात्रे च तद्दानं सात्त्विकं स्मृतम्॥ २०॥

A gift which is bestowed with a sense of duty on one from whom no return is expected, at appropriate time and place, and to a deserving person, that gift has been declared as Sāttvika. (20)

यत्तु प्रत्युपकारार्थं फलमुद्दिश्य वा पुनः।
दीयते च परिक्लिष्टं तद्दानं राजसं स्मृतम्॥ २१॥

A gift which is bestowed in a grudging spirit and with the object of getting a service in return or in the hope of obtaining a reward, is called Rājasika. (21)

अदेशकाले यद्दानमपात्रेभ्यश्च दीयते।
असत्कृतमवज्ञातं तत्तामसमुदाहृतम्॥ २२॥

A gift which is made without good grace and in a disdainful spirit, out of time and place, and to undeserving persons, is said to be Tāmasika. (22)

ॐ तत्सदिति निर्देशो ब्रह्मणस्त्रिविधः स्मृतः।
ब्राह्मणास्तेन वेदाश्च यज्ञाश्च विहिताः पुरा॥ २३॥

OṀ, TAT and SAT—this has been declared as the triple appellation of Brahma, who is Truth, Consciousness and Bliss. By that were the Brāhmaṇas and the Vedas as well as sacrifices created at the cosmic dawn. (23)

तस्मादोमित्युदाहृत्य यज्ञदानतपःक्रियाः।
प्रवर्तन्ते विधानोक्ताः सततं ब्रह्मवादिनाम्॥ २४॥

Therefore, acts of sacrifice, charity and austerity, as enjoined by sacred precepts, are always commenced by noble persons, used to the recitation of Vedic chants, with the invocation of the divine name 'OṀ'. (24)

तदित्यनभिसन्धाय फलं यज्ञतपःक्रियाः।
दानक्रियाश्च विविधाः क्रियन्ते मोक्षकाङ्क्षिभिः॥ २५॥

With the idea that all this belongs to God, who is denoted by the appellation 'TAT', acts of sacrifice and austerity as well as acts of charity of various kinds, are performed by the seekers of liberation, expecting no return for them. (25)

सद्भावे साधुभावे च सदित्येतत्प्रयुज्यते।
प्रशस्ते कर्मणि तथा सच्छब्दः पार्थ युज्यते॥ २६॥

The name of God, 'SAT', is used in the sense of reality and goodness. And the word 'SAT' is also used in the sense of a praiseworthy, auspicious action, Arjuna. (26)

यज्ञे तपसि दाने च स्थितिः सदिति चोच्यते।
कर्म चैव तदर्थीयं सदित्येवाभिधीयते॥ २७॥

And steadfastness in sacrifice, austerity and charity is likewise spoken of as 'SAT' and action for the sake of God is verily termed as 'SAT'. (27)

अश्रद्धया हुतं दत्तं तपस्तप्तं कृतं च यत्।
असदित्युच्यते पार्थ न च तत्प्रेत्य नो इह॥ २८॥

An oblation which is offered, a gift given, an austerity practised, and whatever good deed is performed, if it is without faith, it is termed as naught i.e., 'asat'; therefore, it is of no avail here or hereafter. (28)

ॐ तत्सदिति श्रीमद्भगवद्गीतासूपनिषत्सु ब्रह्मविद्यायां
योगशास्त्रे श्रीकृष्णार्जुनसंवादे श्रद्धात्रयविभागयोगो
नाम सप्तदशोऽध्यायः॥ १७॥

Thus, in the Upaniṣad sung by the Lord, the Science of Brahma, the scripture of Yoga, the dialogue between Śrī Kṛṣṇa and Arjuna, ends the seventeenth chapter entitled "The Yoga of the Division of the Threefold Faith."

Chapter XVIII

अर्जुन उवाच

सन्न्यासस्य महाबाहो तत्त्वमिच्छामि वेदितुम्।
त्यागस्य च हृषीकेश पृथक्केशिनिषूदन॥ १॥

Arjuna said: O mighty-armed Śrī Krṣṇa, O inner controller of all, O Slayer of Keśi, I wish to know severally the truth of Saṁnyāsa as also of Tyāga.(1)

श्रीभगवानुवाच

काम्यानां कर्मणां न्यासं सन्न्यासं कवयो विदुः।
सर्वकर्मफलत्यागं प्राहुस्त्यागं विचक्षणाः॥ २॥

Śrī Bhagavān said: Some sages understand Saṁnyāsa as the giving up of all actions motivated by desire; and the wise declare that Tyāga consists in relinquishing the fruit of all actions. (2)

त्याज्यं दोषवदित्येके कर्म प्राहुर्मनीषिणः।
यज्ञदानतपःकर्म न त्याज्यमिति चापरे॥ ३॥

Some wise men declare that all actions contain a measure of evil, and are, therefore, worth giving up; while others say that acts of sacrifice, charity and penance are not to be shunned. (3)

निश्चयं शृणु मे तत्र त्यागे भरतसत्तम।
त्यागो हि पुरुषव्याघ्र त्रिविधः सम्प्रकीर्तितः॥ ४॥

Of Saṁnyāsa and Tyāga, first hear My conclusion on the subject of renunciation (Tyāga), Arjuna; for renunciation, O tiger among men, has been declared to be of three kinds—Sāttvika, Rājasika and Tāmasika. (4)

यज्ञदानतपःकर्म न त्याज्यं कार्यमेव तत्।
यज्ञो दानं तपश्चैव पावनानि मनीषिणाम्॥ ५॥

Acts of sacrifice, charity and penance are not worth giving up; they must be performed. For sacrifice, charity and penance—all these are purifiers to the wise men. (5)

एतान्यपि तु कर्माणि सङ्गं त्यक्त्वा फलानि च।
कर्तव्यानीति मे पार्थ निश्चितं मतमुत्तमम्॥ ६॥

Hence these acts of sacrifice, charity and penance, and all other acts of duty too, must be performed without attachment and expectation of reward : this is My well-considered and supreme verdict, Arjuna. (6)

नियतस्य तु सन्न्यासः कर्मणो नोपपद्यते।
मोहात्तस्य परित्यागस्तामसः परिकीर्तितः॥ ७॥

(Prohibited acts and those that are motivated by desire should, no doubt, be given up). But it is not advisable to abandon a prescribed duty. Such abandonment out of ignorance has been declared as Tāmasika. (7)

दुःखमित्येव यत्कर्म कायक्लेशभयात्त्यजेत्।
स कृत्वा राजसं त्यागं नैव त्यागफलं लभेत्॥ ८ ॥

Should anyone give up his duties for fear of physical strain, thinking that all actions are verily painful—practising such Rājasika form of renunciation, he does not reap the fruit of renunciation. (8)

कार्यमित्येव यत्कर्म नियतं क्रियतेऽर्जुन।
सङ्गं त्यक्त्वा फलं चैव स त्यागः सात्त्विको मतः॥ ९ ॥

A prescribed duty which is performed simply because it has to be performed, giving up attachment and fruit, that alone has been recognized as the Sāttvika form of renunciation.(9)

न द्वेष्ट्यकुशलं कर्म कुशले नानुषज्जते।
त्यागी सत्त्वसमाविष्टो मेधावी छिन्नसंशयः॥ १० ॥

He who has neither aversion for action which is leading to bondage (अकुशल) nor attachment to that which is conducive to blessedness (कुशल)—imbued with the quality of goodness, he has all his doubts resolved, is intelligent and a man of true renunciation. (10)

न हि देहभृता शक्यं त्यक्तुं कर्माण्यशेषतः।
यस्तु कर्मफलत्यागी स त्यागीत्यभिधीयते॥ ११ ॥

Since all actions cannot be given up in their entirety by anyone possessing a body, he alone who renounces the fruit of actions is called a man of renunciation. (11)

अनिष्टमिष्टं मिश्रं च त्रिविधं कर्मणः फलम्।
भवत्यत्यागिनां प्रेत्य न तु सन्न्यासिनां क्वचित्॥ १२॥

Agreeable, disagreeable and mixed—threefold, indeed, is the fruit that accrues after death from the actions of the unrenouncing. But there is none whatsoever for those who have renounced. (12)

पञ्चैतानि महाबाहो कारणानि निबोध मे।
साङ्ख्ये कृतान्ते प्रोक्तानि सिद्धये सर्वकर्मणाम्॥ १३॥

In the branch of learning known as Sāṅkhya, which prescribes means for neutralizing all actions, the five factors have been mentioned as contributory to the accomplishment of all actions; know them all from Me, Arjuna. (13)

अधिष्ठानं तथा कर्ता करणं च पृथग्विधम्।
विविधाश्च पृथक्चेष्टा दैवं चैवात्र पञ्चमम्॥ १४॥

The following are the factors operating towards the accomplishment of actions, viz., the body and the doer, the organs of different kinds and the different functions of manifold kinds; and the fifth is Daiva, latencies of past actions. (14)

शरीरवाङ्मनोभिर्यत्कर्म प्रारभते नरः।
न्याय्यं वा विपरीतं वा पञ्चैते तस्य हेतवः॥ १५॥

These five are the contributory causes of whatever actions, prescribed or prohibited, man performs with the mind, speech and body.(15)

तत्रैवं सति कर्तारमात्मानं केवलं तु यः।
पश्यत्यकृतबुद्धित्वान्न स पश्यति दुर्मतिः॥ १६॥

Notwithstanding this, however, he who, having an impure mind, regards the absolute, taintless Self alone as the doer, that man of perverse understanding does not view aright. (16)

यस्य नाहङ्कृतो भावो बुद्धिर्यस्य न लिप्यते।
हत्वापि स इमाँल्लोकान्न हन्ति न निबध्यते॥ १७॥

He whose mind is free from the sense of doership, and whose reason is not affected by worldly objects and activities, does not really kill, even having killed all these people, nor does any sin accrue to him. (17)

ज्ञानं ज्ञेयं परिज्ञाता त्रिविधा कर्मचोदना।
करणं कर्म कर्तेति त्रिविधः कर्मसङ्ग्रहः॥ १८॥

The Knower, knowledge and the object of knowledge—these three motivate action. Even so, the doer, the organs and activity—these are the three constituents of action. (18)

ज्ञानं कर्म च कर्ता च त्रिधैव गुणभेदतः।
प्रोच्यते गुणसङ्ख्याने यथावच्छृणु तान्यपि॥ १९॥

In the branch of knowledge dealing with the Guṇas or modes of Prakṛti, knowledge and action as well as the doer have been declared to be of three kinds according to the Guṇa which predominates in each; hear them too duly from Me. (19)

सर्वभूतेषु येनैकं भावमव्ययमीक्षते।
अविभक्तं विभक्तेषु तज्ज्ञानं विद्धि सात्त्विकम्॥ २०॥

That by which man perceives one imperishable

divine existence as undivided and equally present in all individual beings, know that knowledge to be Sāttvika. (20)

पृथक्त्वेन तु यज्ज्ञानं नानाभावान्पृथग्विधान्।
वेत्ति सर्वेषु भूतेषु तज्ज्ञानं विद्धि राजसम्॥ २१॥

The knowledge by which man cognizes many existences of various kinds, as apart from one another, in all beings, know that knowledge to be Rājasika. (21)

यत्तु कृत्स्नवदेकस्मिन्कार्ये सक्तमहैतुकम्।
अतत्त्वार्थवदल्पं च तत्तामसमुदाहृतम्॥ २२॥

Again, that knowledge which clings to one body as if it were the whole, and which is irrational, has no real grasp of truth and is trivial, has been declared as Tāmasika. (22)

नियतं सङ्गरहितमरागद्वेषतः कृतम्।
अफलप्रेप्सुना कर्म यत्तत्सात्त्विकमुच्यते॥ २३॥

That action which is ordained by the scriptures and is not accompanied by the sense of doership, and has been done without any attachment or aversion by one who seeks no return, is called Sāttvika. (23)

यत्तु कामेप्सुना कर्म साहङ्कारेण वा पुनः।
क्रियते बहुलायासं तद्राजसमुदाहृतम्॥ २४॥

That action, however, which involves much strain and is performed by one who seeks enjoyments or by a man full of egotism, has been spoken of as Rājasika. (24)

अनुबन्धं क्षयं हिंसामनवेक्ष्य च पौरुषम्।
मोहादारभ्यते कर्म यत्तत्तामसमुच्यते॥ २५॥

That action which is undertaken through sheer ignorance, without regard to consequences or loss to oneself, injury to others and one's own resourcefulness, is declared as Tāmasika. (25)

मुक्तसङ्गोऽनहंवादी धृत्युत्साहसमन्वितः।
सिद्ध्यसिद्ध्योर्निर्विकारः कर्ता सात्त्विक उच्यते॥ २६॥

Free from attachment, unegoistic, endowed with firmness and zeal and unswayed by success and failure—such a doer is said to be Sāttvika.(26)

रागी कर्मफलप्रेप्सुर्लुब्धो हिंसात्मकोऽशुचिः।
हर्षशोकान्वितः कर्ता राजसः परिकीर्तितः॥ २७॥

The doer who is full of attachment, seeks the fruit of actions and is greedy, and who is oppressive by nature and of impure conduct, and who feels joy and sorrow, has been called Rājasika.(27)

अयुक्तः प्राकृतः स्तब्धः शठोऽनैष्कृतिकोऽलसः।
विषादी दीर्घसूत्री च कर्ता तामस उच्यते॥ २८॥

Lacking piety and self-control, uncultured, arrogant, deceitful, inclined to rob others of their livelihood, slothful, despondent and procrastinating—such a doer is called Tāmasika. (28)

बुद्धेर्भेदं धृतेश्चैव गुणतस्त्रिविधं शृणु।
प्रोच्यमानमशेषेण पृथक्त्वेन धनञ्जय॥ २९॥

Now hear, Arjuna, the threefold divison, based on the predominance of each Guṇa, of understanding (Buddhi) and firmness (Dhṛti), which I shall explain in detail, one by one. (29)

प्रवृत्तिं च निवृत्तिं च कार्याकार्ये भयाभये।
बन्धं मोक्षं च या वेत्ति बुद्धिः सा पार्थ सात्त्विकी॥ ३०॥

The intellect which correctly determines the paths of activity and renunciation, what ought to be done and what should not be done, what is fear and what is fearlessness, and what is bondage and what is liberation, that intellect is Sāttvika.(30)

यया धर्ममधर्मं च कार्यं चाकार्यमेव च।
अयथावत्प्रजानाति बुद्धिः सा पार्थ राजसी॥ ३१॥

The intellect by which man does not truly perceive what is Dharma and what is Adharma, what ought to be done and what should not be done—that intellect is Rājasika. (31)

अधर्मं धर्ममिति या मन्यते तमसावृता।
सर्वार्थान्विपरीतांश्च बुद्धिः सा पार्थ तामसी॥ ३२॥

The intellect wrapped in ignorance, which imagines even Adharma to be Dharma, and sees all other things upside-down—that intellect is Tāmasika, Arjuna. (32)

धृत्या यया धारयते मनःप्राणेन्द्रियक्रियाः।
योगेनाव्यभिचारिण्या धृतिः सा पार्थ सात्त्विकी॥ ३३॥

The unwavering perseverance by which man controls through the Yoga of meditation the functions of the mind, the vital airs and the senses—that firmness, Arjuna, is Sāttvika. (33)

यया तु धर्मकामार्थान्धृत्या धारयतेऽर्जुन।
प्रसङ्गेन फलाकाङ्क्षी धृतिः सा पार्थ राजसी॥ ३४॥

The perseverance (Dhṛti), however, by which the man seeking reward for his actions clutches with extreme fondness virtues, earthly possessions and worldly enjoyments—that persevrance (Dhṛti) is said to be Rājasika, Arjuna. (34)

यया स्वप्नं भयं शोकं विषादं मदमेव च।
न विमुञ्चति दुर्मेधा धृतिः सा पार्थ तामसी॥ ३५॥

The perseverance (Dhṛti) by which an evil-minded person does not give up sleep, fear, anxiety, sorrow and vanity as well, that perseverance is Tāmasika.(35)

सुखं त्विदानीं त्रिविधं शृणु मे भरतर्षभ।
अभ्यासाद्रमते यत्र दुःखान्तं च निगच्छति॥ ३६॥
यत्तदग्रे विषमिव परिणामेऽमृतोपमम्।
तत्सुखं सात्त्विकं प्रोक्तमात्मबुद्धिप्रसादजम्॥ ३७॥

Now hear from Me the threefold joy too. That in which the striver finds enjoyment through practice of adoration, meditation and service to God etc., and whereby he reaches the end of sorrow—such a joy, though appearing as poison in the beginning, tastes like nectar in the end; hence that joy, born as it is of the placidity of mind brought about by meditation on God, has been declared as Sāttvika. (36-37)

विषयेन्द्रियसंयोगाद्यत्तदग्रेऽमृतोपमम्।
परिणामे विषमिव तत्सुखं राजसं स्मृतम्॥ ३८॥

The delight which ensues from the contact of the senses with their objects is eventually poison-like, though appearing at first as nectar; hence it has been spoken of as Rājasika. (38)

यदग्रे चानुबन्धे च सुखं मोहनमात्मनः।
निद्रालस्यप्रमादोत्थं तत्तामसमुदाहृतम्॥ ३९॥

That which stupefies the Self during its enjoyment as well as in the end—derived from sleep, indolence and obstinate error, such delight has been called Tāmasika. (39)

न तदस्ति पृथिव्यां वा दिवि देवेषु वा पुनः।
सत्त्वं प्रकृतिजैर्मुक्तं यदेभिः स्यात्त्रिभिर्गुणैः॥ ४०॥

There is no being on earth, or in the middle region or even among the gods or anywhere else, who is free from these three Guṇas, born of Prakṛti. (40)

ब्राह्मणक्षत्रियविशां शूद्राणां च परन्तप।
कर्माणि प्रविभक्तानि स्वभावप्रभवैर्गुणैः॥ ४१॥

The duties of the Brāhmaṇas, the Kṣatriyas and the Vaiśyas, as well as of the Śūdras have been assigned according to their innate modes of Prakṛti (Guṇas), Arjuna. (41)

शमो दमस्तपः शौचं क्षान्तिरार्जवमेव च।
ज्ञानं विज्ञानमास्तिक्यं ब्रह्मकर्म स्वभावजम्॥ ४२॥

Subjugation of the mind and senses, enduring hardships for the discharge of one's sacred obligations, external and internal purity, forgiving the faults of others, straightness of mind, senses and behaviour, belief in the Vedas and other scriptures, God and life after death etc., study and teaching of the Vedas and other scriptures and realization of the truth relating to God—all these constitute the natural duties of a Brāhmaṇa.(42)

शौर्यं तेजो धृतिर्दाक्ष्यं युद्धे चाप्यपलायनम्।
दानमीश्वरभावश्च क्षात्रं कर्म स्वभावजम्॥ ४३॥

Heroism, majesty, firmness, diligence and dauntlessness in battle, bestowing gifts, and lordliness—all these constitute the natural duty of a Kṣatriya. (43)

कृषिगौरक्ष्यवाणिज्यं वैश्यकर्म स्वभावजम्।
परिचर्यात्मकं कर्म शूद्रस्यापि स्वभावजम्॥ ४४॥

Agriculture, rearing of cows and honest exchange of merchandise—these constitute the natural duty of a Vaiśya (a member of the trading class); and service of the other classes is the natural duty even of a Śūdra (a member of the labouring class). (44)

स्वे स्वे कर्मण्यभिरतः संसिद्धिं लभते नरः।
स्वकर्मनिरतः सिद्धिं यथा विन्दति तच्छृणु॥ ४५॥

Keenly devoted to his own natural duty, man attains the highest perfection in the form of God-realization. Hear the mode of performance whereby the man engaged in his inborn duty reaches that highest consummation. (45)

यतः प्रवृत्तिर्भूतानां येन सर्वमिदं ततम्।
स्वकर्मणा तमभ्यर्च्य सिद्धिं विन्दति मानवः॥ ४६॥

From whom all beings come into being and by whom the whole universe is pervaded, by worshipping Him through the performance of his own natural duties, man attains the highest perfection. (46)

श्रेयान्स्वधर्मो विगुणः परधर्मात्स्वनुष्ठितात्।
स्वभावनियतं कर्म कुर्वन्नाप्नोति किल्बिषम्॥ ४७॥

Better is one's own duty, though devoid of merit, than the duty of another well-performed; for, performing the duty ordained by his own nature, man does not incur sin. (47)

सहजं कर्म कौन्तेय सदोषमपि न त्यजेत्।
सर्वारम्भा हि दोषेण धूमेनाग्निरिवावृताः॥ ४८॥

Therefore, Arjuna, one should not relinquish one's innate duty, even though it has a measure of evil; for all undertakings are beset by some evil, as is the fire covered by smoke. (48)

असक्तबुद्धिः सर्वत्र जितात्मा विगतस्पृहः।
नैष्कर्म्यसिद्धिं परमां सन्न्यासेनाधिगच्छति॥ ४९॥

He whose intellect is unattached everywhere, whose thirst for enjoyment has altogether disappeared and who has subdued his mind, reaches through Sāṅkhyayoga (the path of Knowledge) the consummation of actionlessness. (49)

सिद्धिं प्राप्तो यथा ब्रह्म तथाप्नोति निबोध मे।
समासेनैव कौन्तेय निष्ठा ज्ञानस्य या परा॥ ५०॥

Arjuna, know from Me only briefly the process

through which man having attained actionlessness, which is the highest consummation of Jñānayoga (the path of Knowledge), reaches Brahma. (50)

बुद्ध्या विशुद्धया युक्तो धृत्यात्मानं नियम्य च।
शब्दादीन्विषयांस्त्यक्त्वा रागद्वेषौ व्युदस्य च॥ ५१॥
विविक्तसेवी लघ्वाशी यतवाक्कायमानसः।
ध्यानयोगपरो नित्यं वैराग्यं समुपाश्रितः॥ ५२॥
अहङ्कारं बलं दर्पं कामं क्रोधं परिग्रहम्।
विमुच्य निर्ममः शान्तो ब्रह्मभूयाय कल्पते॥ ५३॥

Endowed with a pure intellect and partaking of a light, Sāttvika and regulated diet, living in a lonely and undefiled place, having rejected sound and other objects of sense, having controlled the mind, speech and body by restraining the mind and senses through firmness of a Sāttvika type, taking a resolute stand on dispassion, after having completely got rid of attraction and aversion and remaining ever devoted to the Yoga of meditation, having given up egotism, violence, arrogance, lust, anger and luxuries, devoid of the feeling of meum and tranquil of heart—such a man becomes qualified for oneness with Brahma, who is Truth, Consciousness and Bliss. (51—53)

ब्रह्मभूतः प्रसन्नात्मा न शोचति न काङ्क्षति।
समः सर्वेषु भूतेषु मद्भक्तिं लभते पराम्॥ ५४॥

Established in identity with Brahma (who is Truth, Consciousness and Bliss solidified), and cheerful in mind, the Sāṅkhyayogī no longer grieves nor craves for anything. The same to all beings, such a Yogī attains supreme devotion to Me. (54)

भक्त्या मामभिजानाति यावान्यश्चास्मि तत्त्वतः।
ततो मां तत्त्वतो ज्ञात्वा विशते तदनन्तरम्॥ ५५॥

Through that supreme devotion he comes to know Me in reality, what and who I am; and thereby knowing Me truly, he forthwith merges into My being. (55)

सर्वकर्माण्यपि सदा कुर्वाणो मद्व्यपाश्रयः।
मत्प्रसादादवाप्नोति शाश्वतं पदमव्ययम्॥ ५६॥

The Karmayogī, however, who depends on Me, attains by My grace the eternal, imperishable state, even though performing all actions. (56)

चेतसा सर्वकर्माणि मयि सन्न्यस्य मत्परः।
बुद्धियोगमुपाश्रित्य मच्चित्तः सततं भव॥ ५७॥

Mentally dedicating all your actions to Me, and taking recourse to Yoga in the form of even-mindedness, be solely devoted to Me and constantly fix your mind on Me. (57)

मच्चित्तः सर्वदुर्गाणि मत्प्रसादात्तरिष्यसि।
अथ चेत्त्वमहङ्कारान्न श्रोष्यसि विनङ्क्ष्यसि॥ ५८॥

With your mind thus devoted to Me, you shall, by My grace overcome all difficulties. But, if from self-conceit you do not care to listen to Me, you will be lost. (58)

यदहङ्कारमाश्रित्य न योत्स्य इति मन्यसे।
मिथ्यैष व्यवसायस्ते प्रकृतिस्त्वां नियोक्ष्यति॥ ५९॥

If, taking your stand on egotism, you think, "I will not fight," vain is this resolve of yours; nature will drive you to the act. (59)

स्वभावजेन कौन्तेय निबद्धः स्वेन कर्मणा।
कर्तुं नेच्छसि यन्मोहात्करिष्यस्यवशोऽपि तत्॥ ६०॥

That action, too, which you are not willing to undertake through ignorance you will perforce perform, bound by your own duty born of your nature. (60)

ईश्वरः सर्वभूतानां हृद्देशेऽर्जुन तिष्ठति।
भ्रामयन्सर्वभूतानि यन्त्रारूढानि मायया॥ ६१॥

Arjuna, God abides in the heart of all creatures, causing them to revolve according to their Karma by His illusive power (Māyā) as though mounted on a machine. (61)

तमेव शरणं गच्छ सर्वभावेन भारत।
तत्प्रसादात्परां शान्तिं स्थानं प्राप्स्यसि शाश्वतम्॥ ६२॥

Take refuge in Him alone with all your being, Arjuna. By His mere grace you will attain supreme peace and the eternal abode. (62)

इति ते ज्ञानमाख्यातं गुह्याद्गुह्यतरं मया।
विमृश्यैतदशेषेण यथेच्छसि तथा कुरु॥ ६३॥

Thus, has this wisdom, the most profound secret of all secret knowledge, been imparted to you by Me; deeply pondering over it, now do as you like. 63)

सर्वगुह्यतमं भूयः शृणु मे परमं वचः।
इष्टोऽसि मे दृढमिति ततो वक्ष्यामि ते हितम्॥ ६४॥

Hear, again, My supremely profound words, the most esoteric of all truths; as you are extremely dear to Me, therefore, I shall give you this salutary advice for your own good. (64)

मन्मना भव मद्भक्तो मद्याजी मां नमस्कुरु।
मामेवैष्यसि सत्यं ते प्रतिजाने प्रियोऽसि मे॥ ६५॥

Give your mind to Me, be devoted to Me, worship Me and bow to Me. Doing so, you will come to Me alone, I truly promise you; for, you are exceptionally dear to Me. (65)

सर्वधर्मान्परित्यज्य मामेकं शरणं व्रज।
अहं त्वा सर्वपापेभ्यो मोक्षयिष्यामि मा शुचः॥ ६६॥

Resigning all your duties to Me, the all-powerful and all supporting Lord, take refuge in Me alone; I shall absolve you of all sins, worry not. (66)

इदं ते नातपस्काय नाभक्ताय कदाचन।
न चाशुश्रूषवे वाच्यं न च मां योऽभ्यसूयति॥ ६७॥

This secret gospel of the Gītā should never be imparted to a man who lacks in austerity, nor to him who is wanting in devotion, nor even to him who is not willing to hear; and in no case to him who finds fault with Me. (67)

य इमं परमं गुह्यं मद्भक्तेष्वभिधास्यति।
भक्तिं मयि परां कृत्वा मामेवैष्यत्यसंशयः॥ ६८॥

He who, offering the highest love to Me, preaches the most profound gospel of the Gītā among My devotees, shall come to Me alone; there is no doubt about it. (68)

न च तस्मान्मनुष्येषु कश्चिन्मे प्रियकृत्तमः।
भविता न च मे तस्मादन्यः प्रियतरो भुवि॥ ६९॥

Among men there is none who does Me a more loving service than he; nor shall anyone be dearer to Me on the entire globe than he. (69)

अध्येष्यते च य इमं धर्म्यं संवादमावयोः।
ज्ञानयज्ञेन तेनाहमिष्टः स्यामिति मे मतिः॥ ७०॥

Whosoever studies this sacred dialogue of ours in the form of the Gītā, by him too shall I be worshipped with Yajña of Knowledge; such is My conviction. (70)

श्रद्धावाननसूयश्च शृणुयादपि यो नरः।
सोऽपि मुक्तः शुभाँल्लोकान्प्राप्नुयात्पुण्यकर्मणाम्॥ ७१॥

The man who listens to the holy Gītā with reverence, being free from malice, he too, liberated from sin, shall reach the propitious worlds of the virtuous. (71)

कच्चिदेतच्छ्रुतं पार्थ त्वयैकाग्रेण चेतसा।
कच्चिदज्ञानसम्मोहः प्रनष्टस्ते धनञ्जय॥ ७२॥

Have you, O Arjuna, heard this gospel of the

Gītā attentively? And has your delusion born of ignorance been destroyed, O Dhanañjaya, conqueror of riches? (72)

अर्जुन उवाच

नष्टो मोहः स्मृतिर्लब्धा त्वत्प्रसादान्मयाच्युत।
स्थितोऽस्मि गतसन्देहः करिष्ये वचनं तव॥ ७३॥

Arjuna said: Kṛṣṇa, by Your grace my delusion has been destroyed and I have gained wisdom. I am free of all doubt. I will do your bidding.(73)

सञ्जय उवाच

इत्यहं वासुदेवस्य पार्थस्य च महात्मनः।
संवादमिममश्रौषमद्भुतं रोमहर्षणम्॥ ७४॥

Sañjaya said: Thus I heard the mysterious and thrilling conversation between Śrī Kṛṣṇa and the high-souled Arjuna, son of Kuntī. (74)

व्यासप्रसादाच्छ्रुतवानेतद्गुह्यमहं परम्।
योगं योगेश्वरात्कृष्णात्साक्षात्कथयतः स्वयम्॥ ७५॥

Having been blessed with the divine vision by the grace of Śrī Vyāsa, I heard in person this supremely esoteric gospel from the Lord of Yoga, Śrī Kṛṣṇa Himself, imparting it to Arjuna. (75)

राजन्संस्मृत्य संस्मृत्य संवादमिममद्भुतम्।
केशवार्जुनयोः पुण्यं हृष्यामि च मुहुर्मुहुः॥ ७६॥

Remembering, over and over, that sacred and

mystic conversation between Bhagavān Śrī Kṛṣṇa and Arjuna, O King! I am thrilled again and yet again. (76)

तच्च संस्मृत्य संस्मृत्य रूपमत्यद्भुतं हरेः।
विस्मयो मे महान्राजन्हृष्यामि च पुनः पुनः॥ ७७॥

Remembering also, again and again, that most wonderful form of Śrī Kṛṣṇa, great is my wonder and I am thrilled over and over again. (77)

यत्र योगेश्वरः कृष्णो यत्र पार्थो धनुर्धरः।
तत्र श्रीर्विजयो भूतिर्ध्रुवा नीतिर्मतिर्मम॥ ७८॥

Wherever there is Bhagavān Śrī Kṛṣṇa, the Lord of Yoga, and wherever there is Arjuna, the wielder of the Gāṇḍīva bow, goodness, victory, glory and unfailing righteousness will surely be there : such is My conviction. (78)

ॐ तत्सदिति श्रीमद्भगवद्गीतासूपनिषत्सु ब्रह्मविद्यायां योगशास्त्रे श्रीकृष्णार्जुनसंवादे मोक्षसन्न्यासयोगो नामाष्टादशोऽध्यायः॥ १८॥

Thus, in the Upaniṣad sung by the Lord, the Science of Brahma, the scripture of Yoga, the dialogue between Śrī Kṛṣṇa and Arjuna, ends the eighteenth chapter entitled "The Yoga of Liberation through the Path of Knowledge and Self-Surrender."

Oṁ Tat Sat

आरती

जय भगवद्गीते, जय भगवद्गीते।
हरि-हिय-कमल-विहारिणि, सुन्दर सुपुनीते॥ जय०
कर्म-सुमर्म-प्रकाशिनि, कामासक्तिहरा।
तत्त्वज्ञान-विकाशिनि, विद्या ब्रह्म परा॥ जय०
निश्चल-भक्ति-विधायिनि, निर्मल मलहारी।
शरण-रहस्य-प्रदायिनि, सब विधि सुखकारी॥ जय०
राग-द्वेष-विदारिणि कारिणि मोद सदा।
भव-भय-हारिणि, तारिणि, परमानन्दप्रदा॥ जय०
आसुरभाव-विनाशिनि, नाशिनि तम-रजनी।
दैवी सद्गुणदायिनि, हरि-रसिका सजनी॥ जय०
समता-त्याग सिखावनि, हरि-मुखकी बानी।
सकल शास्त्रकी स्वामिनि, श्रुतियोंकी रानी॥ जय०
दया-सुधा बरसावनि मातु! कृपा कीजै।
हरिपद-प्रेम दान कर अपनो कर लीजै॥ जय०

God-realization through Practice of Renunciation

त्यक्त्वा कर्मफलासङ्गं नित्यतृप्तो निराश्रयः।
कर्मण्यभिप्रवृत्तोऽपि नैव किञ्चित्करोति सः॥
न हि देहभृता शक्यं त्यक्तुं कर्माण्यशेषतः।
यस्तु कर्मफलत्यागी स त्यागीत्यभिधीयते॥

Living even the life of a householder, man can realize God through the practice of renunciation. Indeed, 'renunciation' is the principal means for attaining God. Therefore, dividing them into seven classes, the marks of renunciation are being shortly written below.

(1) Total Renunciation of Prohibited Acts

This is non-performance, in anyway whatsoever, through mind, speech and the body, low acts prohibited by the scriptures, such as, theft, adultery, falsehood, deception, fraud, oppression, violence, taking of interdicted food and wrong-doing, etc.

(2) Renunciation of Acts performed for the Satisfaction of Worldly Desires

This is non-performance of sacrifices, charities, austerities, worship and other desire-born actions, with a selfish motive,* for gaining objects of enjoyment, e.g., wife, progeny, and wealth, etc., or with the object of curing diseases and terminating other forms of suffering. This is the second type of renunciation.

(3) Total Renunciation of Worldly Thirst

Honour, fame, social prestige, wife, progeny, wealth and whatever other transient objects are automatically gained by the force of Prārabdha (Karma, which has begun to bear fruit), the desire for their increase should be regarded as an obstacle in God-realization, and renounced. This is the third type of renunciation.

(4) Renunciation of the Habit of Extracting Service from Others with a Selfish Motive

Asking for money, or demanding service from

---

* If under the pressure of circumstance, one is compelled to do an act sanctioned by tradition and the scriptures, which is by nature rooted in desire, but non-performance of which causes pain to anybody or adversely affects the traditional ways of Action and worship, performance of it disinterestedly, and only for general good, is not an act of the satisfaction of desire.

another, for personal happiness; and acceptance of things and service given without one's asking for the same; or entertaining any desire in the mind for getting by any means one's self-interest served by another; all these and similar ideas of getting service from another for the satisfaction of self-interest should be renounced.* This is the fourth type of renunciation.

(5) Total Renunciation of Indolence and Desire for Fruit in the Performance of all Duties

Whatever duties there are, e.g., cultivation of devotion to God, worship of the celestials, service of the parents and other elders, performance of

* If non-acceptance of physical service from another, or offer of eatables by another, where one is entitled to accept such service or offer, causes any pain to anyone, or in anyway hinders the education of the people, in that case, acceptance of service, abandoning selfishness, and only for the pleasure of the offerer of service, is not harmful. For non-acceptance of service done by the wife, son or servant, or of eatables offered by friends and relatives, is likely to cause them pain and may prove harmful, so far as propriety of social conduct is concerned.

sacrifices, charities and austerities, maintenance of the household through the earning of livelihood by means of works assigned according to the Varṇāśrama system, and taking of food and drink, etc., for the body—in the performance of these, indolence and every form of desire should be renounced.

(A) Renunciation of Indolence in the Practice of Devotion to God

Regarding it as the supreme duty of one's life, one should hear, reflect on, read and discourse on the mysterious stories of the virtue, glory and Love of God, who is extremely compassionate, friend of all, the best of lovers, the knower of the heart, and renouncing idleness practise constant Japa, together with meditation, of His extremely hallowed Name.

(B) Renunciation of Desire in the Practice of Devotion to God

Regarding all enjoyments of this world and the next as transient and perishable and hindrances in the path of Devotion to God, no prayer should be offered to God for obtaining any object whatsoever, nor any desire should be entertained in the mind for the same. Also, prayer should not be offered to God for the removal of any trouble even when one is overtaken by it; in other words, the thought should be cultivated in the mind that to sacrifice life is preferable to bringing stain on the purity of Bhakti for the sake of this false existence. For instance, Prahlāda, even though intensely persecuted by his father, never offered any prayer to God for the removal of his distress.

Curse with harsh expressions, such as, "Let the chastizement of God be on You", etc., should not be pronounced even against the persecutor, or one who does any injury, and no thought of counter-injury should be entertained against him.

Out of pride of attainment in the path of Devotion, benedictions should not be pronounced in words, such as, "May God restore you to health", "May God remove your distress", "May God grant you a long life", etc.

In correspondence also, words of worldly interest should not be written. In Mārawārī society, there is a general custom of writing such words of worldly import in the form of prayer to God for obtaining worldly objects e.g., "God is our helper here and elsewhere", "God will advance our sales", "God will bring a good monsoon", "God will remove the ailment", etc. Instead of this, auspicious, disinterested words, such as, "God in His state of Bliss exists everywhere", "Performance of Bhajana is the essence of everything", etc., should be written and other than these no word of worldly interest should be written or uttered.

(C) Renunciation of Indolence and Desire in Connection with the Worship of Celestials

There is God's instruction to offer worship to the celestials, who are worthy of being worshipped, during the time appointed for such worship, according to the scriptures as well as tradition. Regarding the carrying out of God's instruction as one's supreme duty, such worship should be offered to a celestial with enthusiasm, according to the prescribed rules, without expression of any desire for the satisfaction of any worldly interest.

With the object of such worship, words implying worldly interest should not be written on the cash-book, and other books of account. For instance, in Mārawārī society there is a custom on the New Year or Dīwālī day, after the worship of Goddess Lakṣmī, to write many words implying worldly desire, such as, "Goddess Lakṣmī will bring profit", "The store will be kept full", "Prosperity and success will be brought", "Under the protection of Goddess Kālī", "Under the protection of Goddess Gaṅgā", etc. These should be substituted by unselfish, auspicious words, such as, "Śrī Lakṣmīnārāyaṇa, in the form of Bliss, is present everywhere", or "Goddess Lakṣmī has been worshipped with great delight and enthusiasm." Similarly, while writing the daily cash-book, this procedure should be followed.

(D) Renunciation of Indolence and Desire in the Service of Parents and other Elders

It is man's supreme duty to render daily services, in all possible ways, to parents, the preceptor, and other persons who are one's superior in Varṇa, Āśrama, age, qualifications, or in whatever other respect it may be, and daily offer them obeisances. Cultivating this thought in the mind, and abandoning all idleness, disinterested, enthusiastic, and according to God's behests, services should be rendered to them.

(E) Renunciation of Indolence and Desire in the Performance of Sacrifices, Charities, Austerities and other Auspicious Deeds

Sacrifices, e. g., the daily obligatory five Great Sacrifices*, and other occasional sacrifices, should be performed. Through gifts of food, clothing, learning, medicine, and wealth, etc., attempt should be made, according to one's capacity, to make all creatures happy, through mind, speech and the body. Similarly, all forms of bodily suffering should be undergone for the preservation of Dharma. These

---

* The five Great Sacrifices are as follows:—(1) Sacrifice to gods (performance of Agnihotra, etc.); (2) Sacrifice to Ṛṣis (study of the Vedas, performance of Sandhyā and Japa of Gāyatrī, etc.); (3) Sacrifice to the Manes (performance of Tarpaṇa, Śrāddha etc.); (4) Sacrifice to Men (entertainment of guests); (5) Sacrifice to all created beings (performance of Balivaiśvadeva).

duties enjoined by the scriptures should be performed, with faith and enthusiasm, according to God's behests, regarding them as supremely important, wholly renouncing the desire for all kinds of enjoyment of this world and the next.

(F) Renunciation of Indolence and Desire in the Performance of proper Work for Maintenance of the Family through earning of Livelihood

It is God's injunction that the family should be maintained through service to the world by performing duties laid down in the scriptures for the respective Varṇas and Āśramas, even as agriculture, cattle-breeding and trade have been laid down as the works of livelihood for the Vaiśya. Therefore, regarding them as duties, treating profit and loss as equal, and renouncing all forms of desire such works should be enthusiastically performed.*

---

* Works performed by a person in the above spirit, being freed from greed, cannot be tainted by evil in anyway, for in works of livelihood greed is the particular cause which leads one to the commission of sin. Therefore, just as Vaiśyas have been advised at length to give up evil practices

(G) Renunciation of Indolence and Desirein Work for Preservation of the Body

In work for preservation of the body, according to the scriptures, e.g., pertaining to food, dress, medicines etc., the desire for enjoyment should be renounced. They should be performed, according to the needs of the occasion, only with the object of God-realization, regarding pleasure and pain, profit and loss, life and death as equal.

Together with the four types of renunciation stated above, when according to this fifth type of renunciation, all evils and all forms of desire are destroyed, and there remains only the one strong desire for God-realization, it should be regarded as the mark of the person, who has attained ripeness in the first stage of Wisdom.

---

connected with trade in the footnote of the Hindi rendering of Chapter XVIII verse 44 of the edition of the Gītā published by the Gita Press, Gorakhpur, even so men should renounce all forms of evil connected with their respective duties as laid down by the Varṇāśrama system, and perform all their duties, for God's sake, disinterestedly, regarding them as injunctions of God.

(6) Total Renunciation of the Sense of Meum and Attachment with regard to all Worldly objects and Activities

All worldly objects like wealth, house, clothes, etc., all relations like the wife, child, friends, etc., and all forms of enjoyment of this world and the next like honour, fame, prestige, etc., being transient and perishable, and regarding them as impermanent, the sense of meum and attachment with regard to them should be renounced. Similarly, having developed pure, exclusive Love for God alone, the embodiment of Existence, Knowledge and Bliss, all sense of meum and attachment should be renounced for all work done through the mind, speech and body, and even for the body itself. This is the sixth type of renunciation.*

---

* The renunciation of thirst, as well as the renunciation of the desire for fruit, with regard to all objects and activities, have been described above as the third and fifth types of renunciation, but even after such renunciation the sense of meum and attachment for them are left as residues; just as even though Bharata Muni through practices of Bhajana and meditation and cultivation of Satsaṅga, had renounced all thirst and desire for fruit with regard to all objects and

Men who reach the stage of this sixth form of renunciation, developing dispassion for all things of the world, get exclusive Love for God alone, the supreme embodiment of Love. Therefore, they retiring to a solitaty place, like only to hear, and talk about, the stories of God's spotless Love, which reveal the virtues, glory and secrets of God, and reflect on the same, and practise Bhajana, meditation and study of the scriptures. They develop a distaste for wasting even a moment of their valuable time in the company of men attached to the world and indulging in laughter, luxury, carelessness, backbiting, enjoyments, and idle talks. They perform all their duties reflecting on God's Form and Name, only for God's sake, and without any worldly attachment.

Thus through renunciation of the sense of meum and attachment with regard to all objects and activities, development of pure Love for God alone,

---

activities, his sense of meum and attachment for the deer and protection of the deer remained. That is why renunciation of the sense of meum and attachment for all objects and activities has been described as the sixth type of renunciation.

the embodiment of Existence, Knowledge, and Bliss, should be regarded as the mark of one who has attained ripeness in the second stage of Wisdom.

(7) Total Renunciation of subtle Desires and Egotism with regard to the World, the Body and all Actions

All objects of the world being creations of Māyā, are wholly transient, and one God alone, the embodiment of Existence, Knowledge, and Bliss equally and completely pervades everywhere, this idea having been firmly established, all subtle desires with regard to objects of the world, including the body, and every form of activity have to be totally renounced. In other words, there should be no pictures of them in the mind in the form of impressions. And due to total lack of identification with the body, there should be no trace of any sense of doership with regard to all actions done through the mind, speech and body. This is the seventh type of renunciation.*

* Even when there is total negation of thirst of the desire for fruit, of the sense of meum and attachment with

The mental impulses of persons, who attain Supreme Dispassion[1] in the form of this seventh type of renunciation, get totally withdrawn from all objects of the world. If at any time any worldly impulse makes its appearance, the impression does not get firmly established, for exclusive and close union of such persons with Vāsudeva, the Paramātmā the embodiment of Existence, Knowledge and Bliss, constantly remains intact.

Therefore, in his mind, all defects and vices having ceased to exist virtues like Ahiṁsā[2],

---

regard to all objects of the world and all forms of activity, there remain subtle desire and feeling of doership as residues. That is why renunciation of subtle desire and egotism has been described as the seventh type of renunciation.

1. In the person, who has reached the sixth stage of renunciation stated above, there may be, now and then, some slight manifestation of attachment, when there is any special contact with objects of enjoyment; but in the person, who has reached the seventh stage of renunciation, there can be no attachment, even when there is contact with objects of enjoyment for in his conception, except God, no other object remains. That is why this renunciation has been described as Supreme Dispassion.

2. Non-infliction of suffering on any creature through mind, speech and the body.

Truth[1], Non-stealing[2], Continence[3], Abstaining from vilification[4], Modesty, Unhaughtiness[5], Artlessness, Purity[6], Contentment[7], Endurance[8], Satsaṅga, Spirit of Service, Sacrifice, Charity, Austerity[9], Study[10], Mind-control, Sense-control, Humility,

---

1. Statement of facts in sweet words, representing exactly what is realized by the mind and the senses.

2. Total lack of theft.

3. Lack of eight forms of sexual enjoyment.

4. Not to make any damaging statement against anybody.

5. Want of desire for reception, honour, public address etc.

6. Both external and internal purity. (Truthful and pure means of earning gives purity to wealth; food obtained by that wealth imparts purity to food; proper behaviour is purity of conduct; purification of the body through use of water, earth, etc.,—all this is called external purity. Through destruction of modifications like attraction, repulsion, and deception, etc., when the mind becomes transparent and pure, it is called internal purity.)

7. Want of thirst for worldly things.

8. Bearing contradictory experiences like heat and cold, pleasure and pain, etc.

9. Sufferings undergone for the practice of one's own Dharma.

10. Study of the Vedas and other elevating scriptures and practice of Kīrtana of God's Name and glory.

Straightness[1], Compassion, Faith[2], Discrimination[3], Dispassion[4], Living in seclusion, Poverty[5], Lack of doubt and distraction, Cessation of Desires, Personal Magnetism[6], Forgiveness[7], Patience[8], Absence of malice[9], Fearlessness[10], Pridelessness,

---

1. This means straightness of the body and mind, together with the senses.

2. Belief, as strong as in things directly perceived, in the Vedas, in the scriptures and in the sayings of saints, the preceptor and God.

3. Real knowledge about what is true and what is false.

4. Total lack of attachment for anything belonging to any region up to Brahmaloka.

5. Want of accumulation of wealth with the sense of meum.

6. It is that power of superior souls under the influence of which even wicked, worldly minded men generally abstain from sinful conduct and engage themselves in virtuous deeds according to their behests.

7. Lack of desire to inflict any form of punishment on one who does an injury.

8. Not to get upset even in the face of the greatest difficulty.

9. Not to bear malice even against one who is maliciously disposed.

10. Total absence of fear.

Peace*, Exclusive Devotion to God, etc., naturally make their appearance.

Thus through the total lack of desire and egotism in regard to all objects, including the body, constant maintenance intact of identity with God is the mark of the person who has attained ripeness in the third stage of Wisdom.

Some of the virtues mentioned above appear in the first and second stages, but all the virtues make their appearance generally in the third stage. For these are the marks of persons, who have reached very near God-realization, and are the means of attainment of direct knowledge of God. That is why in Chapter XIII of the Gītā (verses 7 to 11) Bhagavān Śrī Kṛṣṇa enumerated most of these virtues as Knowledge and in Chapter XVI (verses 1 to 3) described them as the divine qualities.

Moreover, the scriptural authorities regard these virtues as the common Dharma of humanity. All men are entitled to them. Therefore, depending on God, all should make special effort to develop

---

* Total absence of desires and cravings and maintenance of constant cheerfulness in the mind.

the above virtues in their mind.

Conclusion

In this article it has been said that God may be realized through seven types of renunciation. Among them, it has been stated that, the first five types of renunciation indicate the first stage of Wisdom, renunciations upto the sixth type indicate the marks of the second stage of Wisdom, and renunciations upto the seventh type indicate the marks of the third stage of Wisdom. He, who attains ripeness in the third stage of Wisdom above, at once realizes God, the embodiment of Existence, Knowledge and Bliss. Thereafter he loses all connection with this transient, destructible, impermanent world. Just as the person awakened from a dream loses all connection with the dream-world, even so the person awakened from the dream of ignorance loses all connection with the impermanent world, the creation of Māyā. Though from the point of view of the world, all forms of activities are observed as taking place through the body of that person under the force of Prārabdha, and the world gains a lot by such activities, for being freed from desires, attachment and the sense of doership, whatever the Mahātmā does through his mind, speech and body becomes the standard of right conduct in the world, and from the ideas of such a Mahātmā scriptures are formed, yet that person, who has realized Vāsudeva, the embodiment of Existence, Knowledge and Bliss, lives wholly beyond Māyā, consisting of the three Guṇas. Therefore, he during illumination, activity and sleep, etc., which are the effect of the Guṇas, does not hate them, nor, when they cease, desires for them. For, with regard to pleasure and pain, gain and loss, honour and ignominy, praise and blame, etc., and with regard to earth, stone and gold, etc., he attains an attitude of equanimity. Therefore, that Mahātmā when obtaining a desirable object, or in the cessation of what is undesirable, does not feel delighted, nor does he feel any grief when obtaining an undesirable object, or in the loss of what is dear or desirable. If for any reason, his body is cut by a weapon or he is faced with any other form of extreme suffering, that man of wisdom, established exclusively in